**DO NOT REMOVE
CARDS FROM POCKET**

STUDENT'S GUIDE
TO
GOOD GRADES

by
Maria Orlow

The Wheeler School
Providence, Rhode Island

Wayside Publishing
Concord, Massachusetts

To Dietrich

Grateful acknowledgement is made to A.P. Wodehouse Trust No. 3 for permission to reprint the poem "Caliban at Sunset," originally published in *Jeeves and the Feudal Spirit* by P.G. Wodehouse.

ISBN 1-877653-10-1

CONTENTS

ACKNOWLEDGEMENTS

It is a pleasant duty to acknowledge the many acts of kindness that made this book possible. Phylis Dutwin was the first to suggest that I put the results of my long years of experience in teaching study skills into a book.

Once I began the project, numerous colleagues and friends were unfailing in their encouragement and help. Two stalwart souls read and commented on the entire manuscript. Kate Haigney, a fellow teacher of study skills, gave up part of her Christmas vacation to critique the manuscript. Robert Ritsema made a number of suggestions for stylistic improvements. I am grateful to both of them.

Several experts in specific subject areas have reviewed individual chapters. My daughter, Ingrid Orlow, read and commented on both the English and Foreign Language chapters; Jean Leventhal reviewed Foreign Languages; Judy Poirier and Sharon Wolff helped me with the Mathematics and Science chapters respectively. Lynne B. Latson worked on the graphics. In addition, my students at The Wheeler School field-tested earlier versions of this book.

Last, but certainly not least, this book owes a great deal to my husband. He reviewed the History and Research Paper chapters. He also read various drafts of the manuscript, making suggestions for improvements as well as giving emotional support and encouragement throughout the long writing process.

NOTE TO THE TEACHER

This book is deliberately organized so that it can be used either as a textbook or as a reference guide. A number of its features make it particularly suitable for use as a textbook. It is a comprehensive guide with detailed instructions showing what to do and how to do it in all five of the basic academic areas: mathematics, science, history, English, and foreign languages. In addition, there is a chapter on how to write a term paper.

Each chapter is organized around the tasks required of students during homework, in class, while studying for tests, and in taking tests. This makes it easy to use *Student's Guide to Good Grades* as a reference book as well. Any skill you need can be looked up easily in the table of contents or the index. Teaching your students to do the same will help them reach the goal of becoming independent, self-teaching students. They will always be able to turn to this guide to get themselves "unstuck."

The chapters are self-contained: Only rarely are students asked to turn to another chapter for more detailed instruction on performing a particular task. This form of organization necessitates a good deal of repetition, but the structure has the great advantage of allowing you to present the chapters in whatever order is most appropriate for the students you are teaching. Moreover, as you know, repetition and reinforcement are important in the successful teaching of study skills.

The stress on reinforcing particularly useful suggestions to enhance learning is also the basis for a unique feature of the book that incorporates some of the benefits of programmed learning: The presentation of each particularly useful method that can and should be applied in a number of courses begins with a ❏ and ends with a ◆. If the student is already following this advice, he or she can put a big red check mark in the ❏ and skip to the ◆. This device is extremely motivating, because it allows students to "get credit" for the good behaviors they are already exhibiting, and therefore do not need to be taught again. At the same time, it highlights these very powerful behaviors, increasing the likelihood that the suggestions will be incorporated into the student's "study style."

NOTE TO STUDENTS

As you study this book, you will find that many of the suggestions for improving your school performance are repeated in the various chapters. This is because study skills are the student's tool kit. Like the instruments in any tool kit, some are applicable in many different situations — to all or most of your courses.

To highlight and call your attention to these particularly useful suggestions that you should be following, the beginning of each such suggestion is marked with a ❏ and the end with a ◆. When you see a ❏, you have a decision to make:

SCENARIO I: You *already follow* this procedure. If so, you are doing the right thing. Reward yourself by putting a fat red check mark inside the ❏. Then enjoy the glorious feeling of skipping to the ◆, which marks the end of the suggestion. This is the place where you should start reading again. If you are *not yet* following the procedure go to scenario II.

SCENARIO II: Read the suggestion carefully and start following it right now, so that you will be able to get the satisfaction of putting a check inside the ❏ the next time the item is mentioned. The more ❏ you can check off, the more effective you will be as a student.

CHAPTER I

LEARNING HOW TO LEARN

LITTLE THINGS THAT HELP

1. Have all the school supplies and materials you will need on hand at the time when you need them.
2. Have a good place to study where you will not be easily distracted.
3. In the evening make sure everything you will need for school the next day is packed in your school bag. Put the bag in the same place each night, so all you have to do in the morning is grab it.
4. Make sure you know precisely what the homework is and how your teacher wants you to do it. Write the assignment on your assignment sheet as soon as the teacher gives it.
5. Mark all long-term assignments or tests in **red** in your assignment book.
6. Look through your assignment book before leaving school to make sure that you are taking home **all** the materials (textbook, etc.) that you will need to finish your homework.
7. Review your homework notes for each class five minutes before class begins.
8. Make a special point of reading all directions and test questions slowly and accurately.

Some Honest Answers

Perhaps the best way to start a book on how to be a good student is to give some honest answers to old questions about school and learning.

Question No. 1 *"Why do I have to go to school in the first place?"* School may seem to be a waste of time, especially if you're having difficulties learning, and much of what you're doing may seem to have nothing to do with the rest of your life. School is a requirement for all people, but much of its success does depend on you and your attitude. A school is set up to help you learn — it has the equipment, the tools, the resources, and the people all at your disposal. If you work with it, instead of against it; if you see teachers as your colleagues and not your enemies, you will set yourself up to get the most out of the experience.

Unfortunately, many students fail to take advantage of this opportunity. They sleep-walk through the day, tuning out, complaining, and throwing away their best chance to learn what they'll need to know in the future. Time is too valuable to throw away six hours of a day or more. Using your time efficiently and effectively means taking advantage of those six hours to get the most out of them. Do this, and see how quickly your attitude toward school will change.

Question No. 2 *"Why should I study for a course that I don't like?"* Actually, if you are doing poorly in school there are probably several courses you don't like, so this is a very important question for you.

The answer is that we tend to like what we find interesting and easy. We tend to stay involved in activities that are pleasurable, fun, satisfying. In terms of school work, the more you like a subject, the more willing you are to spend time on it. As a result, you keep getting better at it, and like doing it even more. You have established what is known as a "positively reinforcing circle"; each step in the process reinforces the others, and contributes to overall success.

Unfortunately, there is also a "negatively reinforcing circle." The harder you find a subject, the less satisfaction and more frustration you get from doing it. We tend to think of subjects that give little satisfaction and lots of frustration as uninteresting. So we spend as little time as possible on them. Consequently, performance stays poor. This will not increase your interest in the subject, and you will continue to spend less time working on it. The "negatively reinforcing circle" is complete.

Again, all the parts reinforce each other: If you think the subject is difficult, and therefore think that it is uninteresting, you won't spend much time on it. As a result you cannot improve, and you will continue to find the subject frustrating and boring, etc. It all depends upon your attitude. **An important part to becoming a successful student is to break the "negatively reinforcing circle." You have to find ways to keep yourself involved and spend more time studying subjects that you do not like at first.**

"Futurologists" tell us that our society is changing so fast that we should be prepared to learn a completely new set of job skills at least every ten years. So learning how to learn and becoming self-motivated may be the most important skill a student can learn in school. (Thomas, and Robinson, p. 323)

Question No. 3 *"Why are we going over this again? We had it last year."* A good question, that luckily has an equally good answer. Effective learning strategy involves building on what you already know. The more you know about a subject, the easier it is to learn more. This is why teachers want to make sure that you remember what you learned last year. At the same time, you can find out what you forgot about a subject before going on with new material. Reviews at the beginning of the school year help all students to counteract the forgetting that naturally occurs during the long summer vacation. In addition, such reviews are particularly useful for students who have not learned parts of the subject before, or learned them incompletely. Review is a necessary step before you are introduced to the next level of difficulty.

Question No. 4 *"Why should I work for a teacher I do not like?"* This question is at least to some extent a variation of the second one, and the answer is also similar. Teachers we do not like often teach subjects we do not like; and vice versa. So part of the answer lies in your ability to break the "negative reinforcing circle." You'll be surprised how much less you will dislike a teacher if you are doing better in the subject.

But there is another part to the answer. Part of your preparation for life is to learn to work with all sorts of people. In an ideal world we would always work with people we like, but often we do not get to choose whom to work with, so learning to get along with all kinds of people — such as teachers we do not particularly like — is a useful skill. It sounds stupid, but it's the truth. Besides, if you do not work, you are only hurting yourself, not the teacher. The teacher already made it through school.

Sometimes you can develop a good relationship with the teacher in another area, as an advisor to an extra-curricular activity which you enjoy. That may improve your class relations as well. You might also set yourself the personal challenge of doing well in a course taught by a teacher you don't like. If you think the teacher is expecting you to do poorly in the course, surprise him/her by doing well. Think to yourself, "I'm not going to give that teacher the satisfaction of seeing me do poorly in this course."

Following the instructions in this book and putting in extra effort will certainly help improve your grades. The results might surprise you: Not only are you likely to do well in the subject but you might even like the teacher better because you are doing well in his or her course. As you see, we are back to the "positively reinforcing circle."

Introduction

This first chapter is a general one. It describes the theory of how to become a "can do" student. As you will have noticed from the Little Things That Help section at the beginning, Chapter I shows you a system that will improve your performance in all your courses: you are learning how to learn. Chapter I also has another purpose: to explain the reasons behind the theory, since people are much more likely to take advice, if they know why it is supposed to help them.

You won't always have to use all of the techniques discussed in these pages. The idea is to learn ways to understand and remember the material. **Use as many of these techniques as you need to understand each day's homework**. The subject chapters are arranged according to the tasks that you may be asked to perform in each subject, so that you can use this book as a reference guide. For example, if you are having difficulty with word problems in your math course, look up what to do in the math chapter.

Good grades are no accident. Being a good student is basically a three-part process: 1) learning the material presented in school, 2) remembering that material and 3) getting good marks on tests. It is the marks you get on tests that generally determine your grade in a course, but you cannot do well on tests without learning and remembering what the teacher taught you.

Good students give themselves maximum opportunities to

learn, remember, and do well on tests. At each step of their school experience, they focus their attention on the task at hand, and give themselves many opportunities to review what they have learned. It is obvious that 100% attention helps you to learn, so why do good students review so much?

Without review, people usually forget almost everything they have learned. That is just the way our brains function, but there is a way around this limitation of our brains: frequent, spaced, review (Thomas and Robinson, p. 185). Review is one of the top "secrets" of being a good student; a way to get the most learning out of the time you invest. If you make frequent, spaced review a part of your study-style, you will remember most of what you have learned and do well on tests.

Acting Like a Good Student

As a rule good students act differently than students who are not doing as well in school. Good students set things up so that they give themselves the best possible chance to learn. They **expect** to do quite well in all their subjects. More importantly, they know what they have to do in order to reach those results.

One of the advantages good students have is that they can answer the two big questions that get students "unstuck" when they encounter academic problems: "What is making this passage or problem so difficult for me?" And, "what can I do to make it easier for myself" (Tobias, p. 2). In other words, effective students actively engage in that search for solutions to problems they encounter. If they are still stumped after trying hard to solve their own problems, they know where to get the help they need. In either case, **good students do *not* throw up their arms and quit.**

This same active, "can do" attitude is displayed by good students when they come to class. They have all the materials they need for the class, and have done their homework the night before. This allows them to use the class time to review the homework and get feed-back on how well they understood it. All this helps them to remember what they have learned. Good students also "tune in" to the teacher's introduction of the new homework, which in turn will make doing the homework that night go much more smoothly.

❑Efficient students make it as easy as possible for the teacher to straighten out any problems they had with the homework by writing down specifically what the problem was.◆ They are awake, aware, active, and on top of things; their contributions advance the discussion in class, rather than disrupt the learning process. For successful students everything contributes to understanding and remembering the material being studied. That's why they do well on tests.

With inefficient students, on the other hand, the picture is different. They are not efficient learners, rememberers and test-takers. First of all, inefficient students like successful students want to do well in school, so it is not a matter of not wanting to do well. Inefficient students just do not know how to go about it. They do not set things up for maximum success.

There is a good reason for this. Inefficient students have generally had little experience with successful learning, they are often not surprised when they do not understand the assignment. This situation in turn makes it difficult for such students to put in the extra effort that often makes the difference between understanding and not understanding. They do not ask the two questions that can get them "unstuck" (Tobias, p. 2). They feel, "what is the use, I'm not going to understand this anyhow," so they spend much of their study time spinning wheels and worrying rather than working.

Not having pin-pointed the problem, such students can't ask the teacher to clarify a specific point, instead, they say, "I don't understand." This makes it difficult for the teacher to be really helpful, because he or she has no idea where the problem actually lies and can't spend a large part of the class period finding out. (That would require a one-to-one session with the teacher.) The result is that the student does not get the needed help.

In addition, if you have not understood the homework, or didn't finish it, you get to class the next day without the necessary background to get the most out of the class discussion and the chance for review that it affords. You are less likely to understand the material being covered in class, and therefore find the subject boring and "turn off."

In this "turned off" mode, students do not listen attentively when the teacher introduces new material that will be covered in the homework assignment. Missing the teacher's introduction, in turn, makes the homework harder to do and sets the stage for another cycle of incomplete homework, boredom in class, and little learning.

Under the best of circumstances, students who have "turned off" will be present in body but not in mind. They are poor receivers of the information the teacher is trying to give them, but do not interfere with the learning of others. An even more damaging set of likely behaviors: writing notes, talking to your neighbor, making paper airplanes, etc. keeps other people from learning as well.

The scenario described above annoys the teacher and sets up an adversary situation with him or her that does not contribute to success in school. The stage is set for a poor, not a good learning experience. It is both necessary and possible to break this series of habits and expectations that form the "negatively reinforcing" circle. That is the purpose of this book.

Learning New Ways of Doing Things is Hard Work

But first, before we discuss ways of establishing the positively reinforcing" circle, a word of warning: As John Roebling, the architect of the Brooklyn Bridge put it," Nothing is easy and nothing does itself." That also goes for being a successful student. Changing from being an average, or even a poor student into being a good one requires giving up some long-established and familiar work habits. This is hard to do, since none of us likes breaking our routines even if they have not yielded good results. Another factor is that when you learn how to do anything new, be it playing baseball or studying math, at first the results are likely to be disappointing and frustrating. This is because the various skills involved do not yet function smoothly together.

An excellent example of this is learning how to type with the touch system. At first, you are actually slower and will make more mistakes than you did with the hunt-and-peck system. However, if you keep practicing your skills improve, and in the end you will type much faster and more accurately with the touch system than you ever could with the old hunt-and-peck method. The same is true for study skills. (Incidentally, while you are changing your habits, try to get extra sleep. Learning new skills is exhausting, and when you are tired you cannot work well.)

There are six areas that heavily influence whether a student learns, remembers, and tests well: organization, being prepared, classroom behavior, relationship to the teacher, review, and good test-taking skills. Each of these factors is related to the others, so that improvement in one area can lead to an improvement in a student's performance as a whole. It is in these areas that inefficient students need to change their habits.

The better student you are, the smaller the gap between what you already know and the new lesson. In other words, good students can usually predict the information that will be presented in the new lesson. Less successful students find the gap larger, and therefore more difficult to cross.

The larger the gap, the more difficult the lesson is to learn and the more time and effort will be required to get good results. This means that poor students, with the least understanding of the subject and the poorest study skills have to work much harder and put in more time to get a "C," than "A" students do to get their grades. This sounds totally unfair, and it is, but if you follow the directions in this book in the end you, too, can get good grades with less effort.

The chapters in this book will show how to bridge the gap in each subject. Following all the instructions takes a lot of time, and is probably necessary only in your worst subject — where the gap is largest. The step-by-step, "hands-on" instructions are designed so that students will be able to get the most learning from the study time invested.

You will spend all your time learning and none of it "spinning your wheels." While this will not reduce the amount of time you have to invest to narrow the gap, it will keep you from getting frustrated. You will not be putting in hours and hours and still get poor grades, and as the gap narrows, you will find that you have to spend progressively less time to learn and to remember.

If you are getting C's and would like to improve those grades, this book can show you how. After reading this chapter and doing the "Little Things," study the chapter that covers the particular course you want to improve. Concentrate first on doing any "Little Things That Help" you are not doing yet, then on how to do the homework. Next, proceed to the sections on class work, studying for tests, and taking tests.

Organization

Organization is a plan or structure to follow when doing things. Good students are well organized. They follow a plan when they do their work;

they do not just "wing it." Much of a poor student's activity is unorganized. The poor student's studying is much like getting into a car and driving without a map. It is doing something, but not getting anywhere. On the other hand, when you have a plan and know what to do and when to do it, the results are much better.

Being organized is really being prepared ahead of time. Thinking about a task before you do it sounds as though it involves much more work than waiting until the last minute, but that is not true. If you are prepared to do a task beforehand, you can concentrate on the task itself, and that helps you to do it well. Athletes do the same thing. They get their equipment, learn the rules, and practice long before the actual game starts.

❑ When well-organized students start on their homework, they are prepared; they know what they have to do, what equipment they need to do it, when they have to do it, and how.◆ Poor students may have to spend half an hour calling up various friends to get the assignment, or they do the wrong assignment — the world's biggest waste of time! The preparation part of being organized is actually no more than putting everything in order so that you have the best possible chance of doing a good job. In the long run, it makes things easier, cuts down on frustration, and yields much better results.

At Home

Getting organized should start at home with the creation of an optimal studying environment. This will accomplish two things: first, you won't have to waste any study time thinking of the best place to do it, and second, you will get mentally set to do a good job. This second aspect is much more important than many students assume. Athletes do this sort of mental preparation all the time. For instance, downhill skiers let the entire run appear like a movie in their minds before the actual contest. You can use the same training device to improve your school work.

❑ Begin by setting up a good place to study at home. This should be a non-distracting and work-oriented environment that works **for you**. This means your study spot should have a comfortable chair, a sturdy table or desk, a place to store your materials, and good lighting. Make sure that you do not keep your basketball or other distracting items near by. It should be a place that automatically puts you in the "study mode."◆

The study environment should be non-distracting **for you**. This brings us to the issue of background music — a subject that is a sore point in many families. Parents and teachers generally assume that it is impossible to study well with the radio or tape recorder going full blast. Students, on the other hand, claim that too much quiet is distracting.

Here a bit of honest research is in order. You might work on some subjects better with background music, but music might be distracting for other subjects. You don't want to spend more time listening to the music than on thinking about your homework. You might try listening to instrumental music, so that you won't be tempted to sing along with the lyrics. Try studying with different amounts of noise, and take an honest look at the results in terms of work accomplished and the grades you get.

School Supplies: Your Shopping List

A large part of good organization is having good equipment. We have already discussed the furniture in your study space. Just as important are school supplies. Two factors count here. One is to have the right supplies; the other is to have them ready when you need them.

You should not have to disrupt your studying by running out to get missing items, nor should you have to do very much digging through you school bag during class. One easy motion at the beginning of class should produce the ring book with your homework in it, paper for current class notes, writing materials, and assignment book. The only other thing you should need for each class is the textbook.

You want to reduce the hassle and confusion at the beginning of class and be able to concentrate 100% on what you are supposed to be learning, the assignment for the next day etc. **Try to be as prepared for school as an athlete is for a competition.** Runners do not wait until two minutes before a race to buy their running shoes. You will need:

1 looseleaf notebook (8 1/2" X 11")
2 packages looseleaf paper
a divider for each course
5 or more pencils
2 ball point pens
1 hole punch
1 each red, pink, black, green, and blue felt-tipped pens
1 yellow highlighter
1 ruler

1 pair scissors
1 role tape (preferable magic tape)
1 pack each 3X5 and 4X6 cards
1 box paperclips
1 teacher's plan book or other week-at-a-glance type of calendar book

Finally, you should have a good-size bag to put all of your equipment in. A backpack or shoulder bag will keep all your things together, with room for your personal items as well.

Having all this may seem like a "nerdy" thing to do, but there is nothing "cool" about doing poorly in school, and organization is an important step toward getting good grades. It also makes your life much easier, as you will see.

Constructing A Good Notebook

The next thing to do before school starts is to get your notebook all set up. This does not take long to do (in fact writing and reading about it probably takes longer). You might ask, "why should I think about school before my vacation is over? The answer is that you want to get prepared for a task while the pressure is off, so that you will be ready for it mentally and physically when classes start, and the pressure is on. If school has already started, it is not too late, but the sooner you get set up for efficient studying, the sooner you get good results.

There are immediate benefits from having a well-prepared notebook. It will be easier to take good class notes right away on the first day if your notebook is properly set up, and it sends your teacher the message that you are a serious student, who wants to learn. This message gets the teacher-student relationship off to a good start with relatively little effort on your part.

Now let's turn to the actual construction of the notebook. Fill out a label for each course and slip it into the tab of the divider. Put the dividers into the notebook. At least ten sheets of paper for each course complete the notebook. You will be taking this notebook to school each day. Your homework and your class notes will go into it too.

Planning Your Time

The next part of organization you should think about is planning your study time. If you figure out how you are going to get your work done ahead of time, you don't have to waste any time when you are faced with the work itself. There are really two aspects to planning your time: scheduling your daily study time for each subject and planning ahead to eliminate the "bunching up" of study time before tests and other big projects.

There is no one answer to the question as to when and in what order you should study your subjects. People are different, so you have to experiment a little to find out what works best for you. Some people try to get their hardest subject out of the way first, thinking that they are not as tired then as they will be later on, which means they can give their most difficult subject their best effort. In addition, finishing the hardest subject gives a big emotional boost: the rest of the homework will seem much easier. There is also an argument for tackling the hardest subject while still in school (during a free period or study hall **not** during another course): It may be possible to get help from the teacher or another student.

On the other hand, these arguments can be turned around, and many people like to start off with their easiest subject. Doing the homework in your easiest subject with relatively little effort will make it easier to face the worst subject. You might also try combining the two methods. Start with your hardest subject, but promise yourself that you can quit and do something else after half an hour. Half an hour of honest effort may get you over the hump and make it possible to finish the rest of the assignment either right after the half hour is up, or later.

There are other strategies to help you to get through subjects that are difficult and to get the most out of the time you invest. Giving yourself some sort of reward when you have finished a difficult subject, maybe a fifteen-minute break to kick a ball around, or talk on the phone can do much to keep you working when the going is difficult. Just don't cheat!

Simple scheduling can make a big difference too. Try to vary the type of learning as much as possible, so that the memories you have laid down for one subject do not interfere with those that you are trying to produce for the next subject (Pauk, *College*, p. 54). That means, for instance, that you should study math between English and your foreign language, because it deals with numbers and is much more highly structured than any course that deals mostly with words. By the same token, studying science and math back-to-back is probably not a good idea. Again, the idea is to work with, not against the way your brain functions. Finally, give yourself a boost by putting a big red line through each assignment in your assignment book when you have finished the assignment.

Being organized involves more than finishing your daily homework assignments. There is also a long-range aspect to planning. Good students avoid the "study crunch." ❏To do this make sure that you **write the due dates for long-term assignments, and dates of future tests in red in your assignment book** as soon as you know them.◆ Using red makes major assignments hard to overlook. In addition, when you write the assignment down, try to figure out how much advance work will be required, and note this information in the squares for the appropriate days. Below is a sample section of your assignment book. It is filled in as of October 3, when you found out that the test on chapter 3 will be on Friday, October 7. You decided that this test will require two days of extra preparation.

SAMPLE SECTION OF ASSIGNMENT BOOK

HISTORY   OCT. 3-7

Monday
Tuesday
Wednesday start studying for test ch. 3
Thursday finish studying for test ch. 3
Friday TEST CH. 3 (in red)

This system lets you see at a glance what days of a particular week will present a problem. If you are scheduled to study for two tests on Thursday, do your regular homework, and have basketball practice, you will need to work ahead. Can you do some of your studying for the tests before Thursday? Could you finish some of the regular work for other courses earlier in the week? Incidentally, you should make it a rule, ❏if you have study time left over on any day, to use this time to get ahead in some subject or to review class notes. This tactic helps to even out your study time.◆ Count on at least three quarters of an hour of homework per subject each day.

Day-to-Day Preparation

You can readily see that all this advance organization will help you to be prepared for the actual start of classes. But there is also preparedness in the short-term, day-to-day sense. ❑This starts by **getting to class on time with all of the equipment you will need.** The equipment includes your textbook, completed homework, and your notebook with the necessary writing materials.◆

An easy way to make sure that you are not forgetting anything at home is to ❑ establish a regular routine of putting your materials for each class into your notebook as you finish the homework for each course. At the end of your study time, assemble everything you will need the next day in your school bag and park it in the same place each night. Then you will be able to just grab it in the morning — even if you are not quite awake — without having to worry about what needs to go into it.◆ Of course, if you were able to finish your homework assignment for any of your classes while you were still in school, it is best to leave the "equipment" needed for those courses in your locker.

When as a result of doing these steps you arrive in your classroom on time with all your supplies in order, you can be calm, cool, collected, and able to concentrate. This state of mind is essential to provide you with the best possible conditions for learning — nothing is interfering with your ability to listen to the teacher.

The next stage in short-term preparedness is to ❑ **review your home-work** in the few minutes before the class starts, or, if you can't get there until the last minute, during the time in which the teacher is getting the class to order. Reviewing before class is hard to do, because talking to your friends is more fun, but a few minutes spent with your notes can pay off in big ways. If your friends tease you for this, don't mind, because when a pop quiz comes up, you'll be the one smiling, not sitting there with a look of terror on your face.◆

A short review refreshes your memory and helps you to be "tuned-in" to that day's work. This will make it easier for you to participate in the class discussion and take good notes during class. Both of these activities "recycle" and review what you have learned; as we discussed earlier, this is the basic ingredient of remembering what you have learned instead of forgetting most of it.

In addition to everything else, looking over your homework before class is also a good concentration exercise. If you can learn to concentrate on your notes at a time when there are many distractions all around, you will be able to concentrate that much more easily in testing situations.

Homework Assignments

Homework assignments are inevitable, but no problem. You can stay calm and confident when the teacher explains the next day's homework assignment. You are prepared; you won't miss half the instructions, because you are plowing through your school bag trying to find your assignment book or a pencil to write with. ❏**Write the assignment down as the teacher gives it,** note any special directions, and get clarification of any points you do not understand.◆

However, getting your assignment down correctly is only the first part of the task. You will still have to do your homework. To be properly prepared, you should establish the same kind of regular routine before leaving school as you did for the night before in preparation for going to school the next day. ❏**Check your assignment book for each class before you leave school and place all the materials** — textbook, class notebook, and anything else you will need — **into your school bag.**◆ This should not take more than five minutes, but it will save you a good deal of time when you start to do your homework at home.

Incidentally, if you have a study hall in school, you should go through the same routine of checking at your locker beforehand and taking along everything you will need to do the planned homework during study hall. This way you will waste no valuable study time going back to your locker to collect missing items or, even worse, not doing as much homework as you could because you are missing some vital piece of equipment. (We'll talk about the best way of doing your actual homework assignments in the chapters devoted to the various subject areas.)

Classroom Behavior

Careful organization and preparation will also influence your positive attitude in class. The behavior of efficient students involves being attentive, participating in class, and contributing meaningfully to the discussion.

The efficient student is an active listener, and good note-taker. First of all, active listening means paying attention, and "thinking along," not just passively "soaking up" the class discussion. Needless to say, being a positive participant in this sense is much easier if you have done your homework well.

Students who have not done the homework, or done a poor job of it, will have only a vague idea what is going on in class, and consequently find it extraordinarily difficult to pay attention. You would think that students who have not done their homework would listen twice as hard in class to make up for what they had not done the night before, but it doesn't work that way.

The reason is that the gap between what a student who has not done the homework knows and the lesson the teacher is presenting. It is just too much work to follow a lesson you know little about, so the mind "shuts off," and the student no longer pays attention. At best, such students are a neutral factor in class: present in body, but not in mind.

So, doing your homework well advances you from the status of a "turned off" listener to that of an active participant in class the next day. Active participation means that you can answer and ask questions that help the discussion along. This active interaction with the teacher and other students helps you keep your mind on the subject. It also lets you review the information covered in your homework, letting you know if you have understood it.

In addition, good class participation will lead the teacher to see you as an interested, active student. (As we shall see later, this is an important part of establishing a positive student-teacher relationship.) Before your test grades have had a chance to improve significantly, you may be able to show the teacher in the regular class discussion that you understand the material. This is not a substitute for good test grades, but it may help break the "negatively reinforcing circle" and change it to the "positively reinforcing circle." Not only that, if you are paying close attention, you cannot at the same time be distracting either yourself or others. **Being an active participant is a way of both avoiding negative class behavior and reinforcing positive behavior.** All of this goes a long way toward improving your test grades.

If you have done your homework well, you may also find that the information presented by the teacher in class is already in your homework notes. This means that you only have to take class notes on the material that is **not** in your homework notes. Not having to write much makes it easier to keep up with the teacher than if you try to write everything down. The result will be good notes with which to study for the test.

Relationship to the Teacher

There is a spectrum of student behavior from very positive — the active listener and participant — to very disruptive. **A good relationship to the teacher is a big contribution to being an effective student.** Teaching and learning involve a social situation; both students and teachers react to one another and influence each other's behavior. Most people prefer situations that give them a feeling of success, and teachers are no exception.

Successful teaching is essentially measured by students' learning. Teachers are people, too, and like anyone else, they want to succeed. When a teacher feels he or she is well-prepared and has done everything possible to help students master the material at hand, he or she expects the students to learn it. If some students (from the teacher's point of view) remain unreceptive, disruptive, or set up a confrontation with the teacher, the teacher becomes frustrated. The anticipated success experience has turned to failure, and the teacher is likely to blame the students.

When it comes to power distribution within the classroom, the teacher holds most of the trump cards. Students seldom win confrontations with the teacher. In fact, students really have nothing to gain by setting up confrontations; they hurt themselves much more than they can hurt the teacher. Of course, a student can make the teacher's life uncomfortable, but students can't give the teacher poor grades or force him or her to repeat the course. The teacher has the power to do both.

Even if the instructor doesn't use this power, teachers faced with students who are unreceptive, disruptive, or confrontational can send those students negative messages. They may be nonverbal or even unconscious — a look, the tone of voice, a gesture can get the message across that the teacher thinks, "You are a bad student, you will not do well in this class. In fact, I do not like having you here at all."

The other side to the teacher-student relationship is positive. If a student can contribute to the teacher's feeling of success by being an active listener and constructive contributor in class, his or her presence is likely to result in positive messages, "You are a good student, I like having you in class."

You may ask, of course, why should a student care one way or the other, if the teacher likes him or her? It is strange, but true, that we tend to do well if people expect us to do well. Expectations can get concrete results (Shaughnessy, pp. 275 and 291). Unfortunately, this same relationship can work against the student. If your behavior — lack of preparation for class, disruptiveness, etc. — convinces the teacher that you will not do well in the course, you will generate behavior patterns in the teacher that make it less likely that you can do well. Teachers tend to be less patient, explain things less carefully, and generally interact less positively with you. Poor grades will almost inevitably follow.

Fortunately, research also shows clearly that a teacher who expects a student to do well will act in ways that help the student to do well. For example, the teacher can give more encouragement, explain things more carefully, be more patient. The teacher may even overlook some negative behavior.

Now, the student is by no means a helpless, passive object in the student-teacher relationship. As in any relationship, both parties influence the outcome. The initial step can very well be taken by the student. **Teachers know that doing a good job on the homework, listening actively and participating in class lead to good test scores,** so seeing a student doing these things is likely to convince the teacher that such a student is doing everything that he or she can to do well in the course. It is difficult for a teacher to resist seeing this change of behavior on the student's part and not do everything to help that student achieve academic success.

Review

Doing a good job on homework and in class are necessary to get good grades, but they are only preparation for the most important factor in a teacher's grade book: tests. It is impossible to get good test grades unless you remember the material. Your goal is to learn the material so well by test time, that the pressure of the testing situation will not make you forget what you learned. This is where review comes in. As we discussed before, people normally forget most of what they learn. A regular program of review will help you to remember most of it instead. The least painful way to remember the most is to review in four stages:

❏ *Stage 1* - **(5 -10 minutes) Read over your homework right after you finish each assignment.** Does it still make sense? If your notes or the exercise do not make sense now, go back and correct the assignment.◆

Stage 2 - **(5 minutes) Review the homework before class.** This has already been discussed on pp. 14 and 15.

Stage 3 - **(40 minutes, but not one minute that you do not have to spend anyway) Use class session to review by being an active participant.** This has already been discussed p. 16.

Stage 4 - **(2 separate days) Study for tests.** Being prepared for tests depends on two factors: having enough time to study for each test, and having good materials to study from. If either of these is lacking, it would be a miracle if you do well on the test. Now miracles do happen, but efficient students don't count on them. First of all, go back and reread the section on planning your time (pp. 11 through 14). This is important, not only because you need adequate time to study for each test, but also because you need to avoid wasting your time worrying about the work you are ignoring; if you planned your time well you are not ignoring anything. Also make sure that the test date as well as the days you will need to review for the test are marked in your assignment book.

As for good materials to study from, your homework and class notes are the ingredients. The better they are, the more effective your test preparation will be. The details of actual studying for tests will be discussed in the various chapters, since they are different for each subject. Actually, if you have been properly prepared all along, studying for tests will probably turn out to be easier than you think. You can now reap the benefits of organizing, being prepared, participating in class, and reviewing the material.

Taking Tests

Tests largely determine the grade you get in the course. If you do not do well on tests, you will not get credit for the material you have learned and remembered. So, no book on how to become a better student would be complete without advice on how to improve your test grades.

To do well on tests you must know the material and you must be able to answer the questions in the time given. Like most other aspects of being a good student, test-taking is easier when you know what you are doing and have a plan how to go about doing it. Good test-taking starts with **preparation.** Preparation has two aspects: learning the material and setting up the best possible conditions for taking the test.

With good review you will know the material, so we will concentrate here on the other things you can do to raise your grade. ❏Go to bed early the night before the test, and eat a good breakfast in the morning.◆ If you are tired and/or hungry, you may miss the simplest questions. ❏On test day, get to class in plenty of time with all the materials you will need (several well-sharpened pencils, etc.) and nothing else.◆ If you are well-prepared, you won't be afraid of the test. Now give yourself the best possible chance to get into that calm, cool, confident frame of mind that helps to do well on any task. If there is no clock in your classroom, bring a watch to pace yourself.

Once you receive the test, the preparation phase is over, but, do not rush headlong to fill in the answers. ❏First, you need to set up a way to pace yourself, so that you will answer as many questions as possible in the available time. If your teacher did not indicate the amount of time to spend on each section of the test, you must decide this for yourself. Allow ten minutes at the end to fill in the answers to any questions you did not know and to look over the test. Now write down the time at which you should start each section.◆

Why take valuable test time (about three minutes) to go through this procedure which does not result in a single answer? The reason is that many students spend so much time on the early questions, that they run out of time before they have finished the test, losing credit for answers they knew perfectly well.

❏ Start actually working on the first section of the test by **reading the directions** carefully, one word at a time. Students lose a lot of credit by not following test directions. For example, if you are asked to give synonyms for various words and you give antonyms instead, you will receive no credit for your efforts. If you are allowed to mark up the test, underlining the important words will help to fix your attention on them.

Finally, if any of the directions are unclear, ask the teacher to clarify them. You will help not only yourself, but you may also help someone else who was too shy to ask.◆

Now we come to the test questions themselves. Broadly speaking, tests come in two types: objective, and essay. **Objective questions** come in several forms: multiple-choice, identification, true-false, fill-in-the-blank, complete-the sentence, matching). With this type of question the teacher is asking a large number of questions that deal with a wide range of isolated bits of information. Your job is to recognize as many correct answers as possible when you see them.

Objective questions call for speed. There are many questions to get through within a limited time, so you cannot spend too much time on any one of them. However, doing well on objective questions also requires **accurate reading of both the directions and the questions** themselves.

Since all you are asked to do is to recognize the answer when you see it, teachers often make objective questions a little harder through the language they use in the directions and the questions themselves. Watch out especially for little words that change the meaning of a sentence, and if you are allowed to, underline or circle them, to make them stick out for you. **Do *not* attempt to gain speed by hasty reading.** The way to gain speed in answering objective questions is through **careful preparation and efficient test-taking.**

You have already done all the preparation necessary, so we will proceed to efficient test-taking. After carefully reading the directions, ❏go through each objective section of the test answering all the questions you know right off the bat. Do not stop to think about questions you do not know, just put a check mark in the margin, so you can find the unanswered question quickly when you come back to it, and go on.◆

❏ When you get to the end of a section, use your remaining time for that section (but not more time than you allocated) to go back and answer as many of the checked questions as you can, erasing the check mark when you have answered a question. But again, do **not** spend five minutes thinking about any one of them.◆ Actually, your teacher may help you out. Writing good objective questions is very hard to do, so it is very likely that some questions will give you the answer to other questions. Good students watch for such gifts.

Essay questions do not require as much reading ability on your part as objective questions do, but they call for more actual knowledge and some ability to express yourself in writing. The words used in this type of question are not likely to create a problem in themselves, but you do have to know which question words each subject uses so that you will answer the question that is actually asked. Students lose a lot of credit giving beautiful answers to unasked questions! Write your answer in good, clear English in complete sentences (unless the teacher instructs you otherwise).

Efficiency in writing an answer to this type of question should be gained through good preparation, so that you will know what to write. In addition, you will save time if you can pack a lot of information into a few well-chosen words. Stick to the point, and do not repeat yourself. Do not write a mass of confused sentences and hope that the teacher will find something in your answer. ❑ Avoid repetition, getting off the topic, or leaving something out by making a "mini-outline" of the question (noting the main points you want to cover with just a word or phrase) before you start.◆

Keep to your time schedule. If you know only a little about the subject, express everything you know and leave space to add more if inspiration comes to you before the end of the test. If you cannot think of anything at all, leave a half page so that you can come back to the question and go on. Do **not** spend too much time thinking about these questions, or you will sacrifice credit for later questions that you **do** know. As in the objective questions, use any time you have left to go back and answer, or answer more completely, any question you did not finish.

❑ In the last ten minutes, which you have reserved for looking over your test, **if there is no penalty for guessing** begin by making an educated guess for each blank objective question. If you have no idea at all on a multiple-choice question, choose the second to last answer (statistically, it is used more often than other choices). Then add any information you have thought of to your essay questions. Finally, reread your answers and see if you still think they are correct.◆

❑ One word of warning. **Never change the answer to an objective question unless you are 110% sure that the new version is correct.** Your first hunch is more likely to be right than a second guess, and many people end up changing correct answers into wrong ones!◆

Tests are by far the largest factor in the grade you get in a course, so improving your test grades has a big impact on the grade you get in a course. **The combination of pacing yourself, and accurate reading of both directions and questions can easily raise your test grades by a letter or even more** without any new subject-matter learning. Add careful preparation, so you will actually know the material you are being tested on, and you have the potential for two letter grades!

Conclusion

This is a good point to re-emphasize the relationship of the various parts of being an efficient student. If you are well-organized, it is much easier to do your homework and learn more easily. You will be well prepared for class the next day, which helps you to take full advantage of the teacher's comments and the classroom discussion to review what you learned the night before, as well as listen carefully to the teacher's explanation of the new homework. Students who are receptive and interact positively in class tend to have good relations with the teacher, learn more, remember more, and do better on tests. In short, you will be looked upon as a good student, and you will feel better about yourself and about school in general.

The way successful learning works can also be illustrated by the pyramid to good grades shown on the next page. At each level, you make the tools that will help you be as efficient as possible on the next level. The pyramid gets increasingly narrow. This is to show you how you should allocate your study time: As you go up the pyramid, each level should receive less of the overall time you are involved in school work.

The tasks required on the various levels will be somewhat different for the different subjects (the pyramid shown here is a composite of what is required in the various subjects) but the levels themselves remain the same. The next five chapters are each devoted to a separate subject area and will show you what to do to be a successful student of that subject.

Pyramid to Good Grades

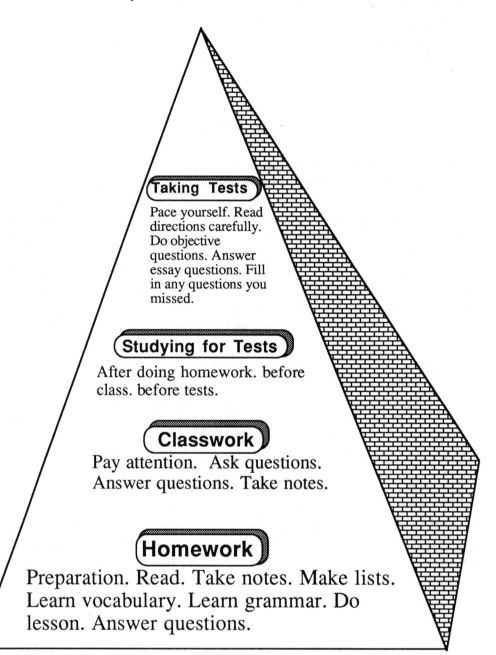

Taking Tests
Pace yourself. Read directions carefully. Do objective questions. Answer essay questions. Fill in any questions you missed.

Studying for Tests
After doing homework. before class. before tests.

Classwork
Pay attention. Ask questions. Answer questions. Take notes.

Homework
Preparation. Read. Take notes. Make lists. Learn vocabulary. Learn grammar. Do lesson. Answer questions.

REFERENCES

Pauk, Walter. *How to Study in College*. 2nd ed. Boston: Houghton Mifflin, 1974.

Pauk, Walter. *Successful Scholarship*. Englewood Cliffs, NJ.: Prentice-Hall, 1966.

Shaughnessy, Mina P. *Errors and Expectations*. New York: Oxford University Press, 1977.

Thomas, Ellen Lamar and Robinson, H. Alan. *Improving Reading in Every Class*. 3rd. ed. Boston, 1982.

Tobias, Sheila. "Insiders and Outsiders." *Academic Connections.* (Winter, 1988).

Tobias, Sheila. *Succeed with Math: Every Student's Guide to Conquering Math Anxiety*. New York: College Entrance Examination Board, 1987.

CHAPTER II

MATHEMATICS

LITTLE THINGS THAT HELP

1. Spend a third of your math homework time studying the teacher's explanation, the textbook explanation and examples **before** spending the other two thirds doing the problems.
2. The mathematics textbook must be read slowly and carefully because **every word** is important. Expect it to take ten times longer than "normal" assignments and allot time accordingly.
3. Do homework on the front of the paper only. Use the back to write the correct version of problems you missed when the teacher goes over them in class. Result: a perfect study sheet for reviews.
4. Show all steps involved in doing each problem both on homework and on tests. Never put down just the answer. Your teacher needs to know where your understanding broke down, and might give partial credit on tests.
5. When you come across something you do not understand while doing your homework, write down the specific question right on your homework to ask in class.
6. During class participate 100% by mentally answering when you are not called on, checking your answer against the one given aloud. Ask the teacher to clear up the problem if your own answer is not correct.
7. Keep all returned homework papers in your notebook.

Tasks and Difficulties in Studying Mathematics

To many students math is like a mystery with seven seals. This chapter (adapted largely from Ellen Lamar Thomas, and H. Alan Robinson, *Improving Reading in Every Class* will try to "break those seals." This may not turn you into a math "whiz kid," but will definitely improve your math grades.

There is however, no denying that mathematics has some built-in hurdles. It is full of abstractions, uses very exact terms, requires precise computation, and math books have many ideas packed into a single page.

Mathematics is certainly abstract, and you have to learn to deal with theories and numbers not directly related to real objects, but math as such is not far removed from our everyday lives. Especially in these times of computers and high tech, we are surrounded with examples of the practical application of mathematics.

Nevertheless, things that "look like they have something to do with math" often scare us and lead us to accept what other people say or write without question (for example the use of statistics in advertising). We also tend to think if a machine has figured it out, it has got to be right — wrong. Even without technical failures, your bill at the grocery store is only as accurate as the checker's punching in of the numbers. Estimating your grocery costs and then checking it against the actual bill could well save you money.

Another scary aspect of math is the attitude that you must get the right answer. The fear of "not getting it right" paralyzes many students, so that they stop thinking and fail to apply what they **do** know to the problem at hand. (Tobias, pp. 2, 4 and 5.)

Mathematicians consider the **process and theories involved more important than getting the right answer**. There is almost always more than one way of doing any problem. If you get stuck, and know the process and theories, you don't need to throw up your hands and quit. You will be able to use what you do remember to approach the problem in another way.

So the best way to improve your math grade is to act more like a mathematician. Learn the process and the theories and view the homework problems as mere examples. That will give you control over the information and allow you to do other problems that are also examples of the same processes and theories.

The language of mathematics can be a stumbling block as well. Mathematical terms are to the mathematician as a scalpel is to a surgeon: a precision tool. Some of the math terms are common everyday words we use in other settings as well (such as "between"), others like "polynomial" will be new. Each of these words, however, has an exact mathematical meaning, and if you do not know what that meaning is, you may fail to understand a whole paragraph or more in your math textbook.

In a sense, mathematics is a language all its own. In fact, it was and still is the world's only universal language. Mathematicians from every corner of the earth could and can understand each other. That is one reason why math words are so clearly defined, and "up front." Even in word problems there is little reading between the lines in math, and no connotations, implications, or emotional overtones.

This one-to-one relationship between a term and what it means lets the mathematician write in a special way too. Because there should be no confusion about what the mathematician is saying, he/she does not need to explain the meaning or try to convey it in several different ways. This leads to a very "compact" style of writing with many important ideas packed into each page, or even paragraph.

In comparison to English class, the number of pages you are assigned for homework in math will be few. Because so many ideas are packed into so few words, you have to **read math at about one tenth the speed with which you would read a novel**. However, studying your teacher's explanation and that of the textbook is only a third of your homework job. The other two thirds of your time should be spent doing the assigned problems.

Finally, math is also very cumulative. What you learn on any given day, you will need for the rest of the course. So you can never say, "the test is over, I don't have to worry about that information any more!" This aspect of math gives great rewards to students who do their daily homework diligently and review frequently; the penalties for those who do not do these things are correspondingly heavy.

Mathematics requires more precision than most of your other subjects — science is the only other subject that comes close — but the levels of the good grade pyramid (next page) and the way you should allocate your time among the various levels is the same as for other courses. Spend the most time at the bottom of the pyramid, the homework level, otherwise the higher levels will not have the support they need, and the whole pyramid will collapse. To make it easy for you to orient yourself within the chapter, the levels appear in bold print.

Pyramid to Good Grades in Math

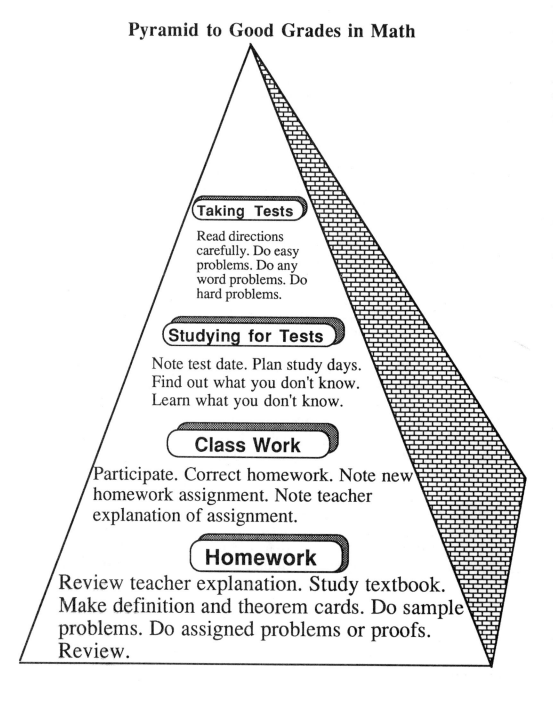

Taking Tests

Read directions carefully. Do easy problems. Do any word problems. Do hard problems.

Studying for Tests

Note test date. Plan study days. Find out what you don't know. Learn what you don't know.

Class Work

Participate. Correct homework. Note new homework assignment. Note teacher explanation of assignment.

Homework

Review teacher explanation. Study textbook. Make definition and theorem cards. Do sample problems. Do assigned problems or proofs. Review.

Homework

This section of chapter 3 is divided into four parts: 1) studying the textbook, 2) algebra, 3) word problems, and 4) geometry. Start with the part on studying the textbook, since this is important in all math courses. Next, concentrate on the parts of math that apply to you. Each part is clearly labeled in italics to make it easy for you to find the part on which you want to work.

Part 1 — Studying the Textbook

You will save time and effort by spending the first third of your math homework time learning what the assignment is all about. Doing the assigned problems first thing is like getting into a car and driving to a place where you have never been before without looking up the route on the map before you start. You may accidentally get to where you want to go, but it will certainly not be by the quickest route.

Modern math textbooks, with their do-it-yourself formats, are set up to make learning the math theory easy for you. If your teacher has given you a detailed introduction to the assignment, review that before you study the textbook explanation. That way, you will already know most of what the textbook will tell you, and it will be quicker and easier to understand.

The formula for success in studying math textbook explanations is to give them **three** readings. Not even math scholars digest all the information in one reading, so do not expect the impossible of yourself. This sounds like a lot of extra work, but it is actually a labor-saving device: It helps you learn and remember the most in the shortest time. Investing time in studying the textbook explanation speeds up doing the problems later.

Step 1 - First reading
The object of this reading is to get a general idea of what the lesson is about and to remove the reading road blocks of unknown words. Using medium speed, read through the explanation. Do not stop to puzzle out words you do not know; just underline them in pencil if the book is yours, if not, write them on a separate sheet of paper. As you read, try to relate the new material to what you already know: How is it the same? How is it different?

Next, read the words you have underlined (or written on a separate sheet of paper) by applying the system for reading unknown words described in Chapter 3 (Science pp. 57–61). Do not neglect this part of reading the assignment. The condensed style of writing in math means that you need to read every single word accurately to get the author's full meaning.

Finally, make a 3x5 definition card for each of the bold print terms that are in your assignment. These terms are the precision tools of math, and you will need them forever after, so a clear understanding when you first come into contact with them saves you time and effort later. Good math students learn such terms automatically, and so they do not need this extra memory crutch, but if you are not getting "A's" in math and want to improve your grade, making the extra effort at this point is well worth your while.

Write the term on the front of the card and the definition on the back. Make a drawing of the concept if possible. Another trick that makes math concepts easier to remember: figure out and write a non-example (what this concept does not include). Adding a drawing of the non-example is even better. The advantage of this trick is to make the concept that much clearer in your mind. Like the sample below, you should have three things on the back of your 3x5 card: the definition, a drawing, and a non-example.

SAMPLE 3X5 DEFINITION CARD
front

equilateral triangle

SAMPLE 3X5 DEFINITION CARD
back

definition: a triangle with 3 sides of equal length
$(a = b = c)$

drawing:

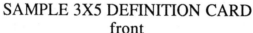

non-example: can **not** be a right triangle

Step 2 - Second, in-depth reading

The easiest way to do the second reading is to read each word slowly, aloud if possible. The slowest readers tend to understand the most math in the shortest time, so don't practice speed reading on your math assignment. Reading aloud slows you down, and many people also find it easier to understand a math text if they can hear as well as see the words.

Since learning each new theorem or concept in math assumes mastery of whatever you learned before, stop at the end of each sentence, mark your place with an empty 3x5 card, and think about what the sentence means. You should spend as much time thinking about the meaning as you do reading the actual words.

If you cannot honestly say you know what the sentence means, reread the sentence. The success of detailed reading depends on knowing the meaning of each word. If there are any words you aren't completely sure of, look them up in the index of your textbook. The index will give you the page number where each math term was first explained. Study the explanation before continuing your in-depth reading. (For non-math words, you may have to consult a dictionary.)

If there are any drawings or figures in the explanation, use the back-and-forth method of reading described in Chapter III (pp. 61–62). If there are no drawings, try making some of your own on a piece of scrap paper to aid your understanding. Mathematicians use this method to make the words more concrete (they call it "visualizing"), and so can you. It gives you an extra "hook" on which to hang the concept.

Step 3 - Quick reading

As a last step, give the passage a quick overall reading. This will enable you to fit the details that you have concentrated on in the second reading into the larger picture the textbook authors have been trying to develop.

Now that you know how to study the textbook, let us turn to algebra.

Part 2 — Algebra

Step 1 - ❑ Check your assignment sheet and study any teacher explanation of the assignment.

As in all subjects, the first thing to do when you start your algebra homework is to check your assignment sheet. Make sure you are doing the correct assignment and be certain to read any explanation the teacher gave of the assignment.◆

Step 2 - **Study the textbook.**

Use the system described in PART 1 (pp. 31-33) to study the textbook explanation. If you give in to the temptation of starting on the problems before you have read the explanation, it will take you much longer in the end, and you will be much more frustrated!

Step 3 - **Do the first sample problem.**

Next, check your understanding of the textbook explanation by doing the first sample problem. Use pencil in doing any math, so that corrections are easily made. Cover up the steps that are printed in the textbook. When you have finished each one, uncover that step in the sample problem and check to see if you are correct. If your step matches that of the book, go on to the next one. If it does **not** match the book, go back to the textbook explanation to clear up your misunderstanding. Correct your work and continue with the next step until you reach the end of the sample problem.

One word of warning — if you do not understand why the author did every step in each of the sample problems, be sure to make an appointment to see your teacher. This means that you are having difficulties at a very basic level, which need to be cleared up right away. Math is so cumulative that a basic misunderstanding here is going to come back and haunt you again and again. If you are having problems at this point you will probably need more help than is available during a class session, so do not hesitate to ask your teacher for some extra time. Most teachers want their students to succeed in their courses and will do anything in their power to achieve that outcome. One half-hour session can often work wonders, so it is dumb **not** to ask for help if you need it.

Step 4 - **Solve the assigned problems that are like the first sample problem.**

High school algebra books are set up so that the first problems will be like the first sample problem. The only difference is the numbers and letters used in the assigned problems. If you were able to do the first sample problem, you should be able to do these problems easily. To make sure that you are doing everything correctly, check each step with the sample problem for at least the first couple of problems.

To get the most learning out of your efforts, and to provide yourself with a handy study guide to prepare for quizzes and tests, do the assigned problems on the front of your paper and use the back to write down the correct version of any problems you did not do correctly on the homework. You will have a perfect record of all the problems you were assigned for homework, how to do each one, and with which problems you had trouble.

Work on one problem at a time; copy the problem carefully, writing the numbers extra clearly. Then check the textbook to make sure you copied the problem 100% accurately. These simple measures eliminate two common sources of error: mistaking one number for another, and copying the problem inaccurately.

Now go ahead and solve your problem. Be sure to follow the pattern of steps shown in the sample problem and to show your work for every step. You cannot afford to take short cuts until you are a super math student. The reason is that your teacher needs to see all the steps you have performed in order to know where the trouble is if you do not understand the lesson perfectly. If you get to class and say, "I don't understand the lesson," the teacher has no way to "zero in" on your problem. So make it as easy as possible for both your teacher and yourself to pinpoint any difficulties you might have by showing all your work.

When you encounter a problem you can not do easily, do not panic, and do not throw up your hands and quit. The best learning strategy at this point is to **get as far as you possibly can on your own before asking for help or quitting**. If you figure things out on your own, and have to think hard to do it, you are much less likely to forget them than if you have the information handed to you. Also, by helping yourself out of a jam, you might learn a method to help get you "unstuck" the next time. The trick is to get yourself to do that. Knowing what to do in case of trouble is a good way to keep yourself going. So if you have difficulty, go back to the sample problem doing each step with the numbers and letters from your actual homework problem substituted for the ones in the sample.

If this does not help, try going back to the last problem you solved correctly and compare it to the one with which you are having difficulty. See if you can figure out what it is that makes this new problem harder. (For example, it may be something simple like more difficult numbers). In case neither of these "tricks" help, try doing another assignment for a while and give your algebra another try at a later time. A fresh start may clear your mind and let you think along different paths and thus straighten out the earlier difficulty. If you are still stuck after trying all these strategies, write your question on your home work paper and ask your teacher for help in class the next day.

Step 5 - **Check your answer**.
This step is easy, but often omitted: If the answers are printed in the

back of the textbook, check each problem as you finish it. Remember: the process of arriving at the answer is more important than the answer itself. If there no answers in the book, check yourself by substituting your answer for the unknown(s) to see if it is correct. If your answer is **not** correct, you need to find out where your error is before going on to the next problem. Go back to the sample problem and compare.

Step 6 - **Repeat steps 3-5 with each of the other sample problems and the assigned problems like them**.

When you have done all the assigned problems that are like the first sample problem, repeat steps 3-5 with the next sample problem and the assigned problems like it. Keep recycling steps 3-5 until you have done all the sample problems and the assigned problems like them. The above steps will probably take care of all the assigned problems in the first two sections.

Step 7 - **Do the rest of the assigned problems**.

Students are often also assigned some of the more difficult problems at the end of the lesson. These problems apply and expand the theory that you have learned in the lesson. Take at least a stab at these. They should not be so mysterious if you have understood the lesson and done the preceding problems correctly. In fact, you'll be surprised at how easy they are.

Step 8 - **Review the assignment**.

You may now breathe a sigh of relief, but don't call your work done just yet. ❏ You will get the most learning out of the time spent studying if you spend just five more minutes at this point with a review. Figure out how the problems you have just done fit into what you already know about algebra. Did you learn a new way to simplify or solve problems? ◆

Follow the steps repeated below on your next assignment and you will see how following a plan and investing the necessary time produces homework that is thoroughly done. Rather than just going through the motions, you have done some real work, and learned something in the process. When you get to class, you will know what is going on, and you can use the time to reinforce your learning. You are more likely to waste your class time being bored or lost if you did not do your homework thoroughly, and class time is time you can not afford to waste.

Step 1 - Check your assignment sheet and study any teacher explanation of the assignment.

Step 2 - Study the textbook explanation.

Step 3 - Do first sample problem.

Step 4 - Solve the assigned problems that are like the first sample problem.

Step 5 - Check your answer.

Step 6 - When you have finished all the problems like sample problem 1, repeat steps 3-5 with each of the other sample problems and the assigned problems like them.

Step 7 - Do the rest of the assigned problems.

Step 8 - Review the assignment.

Part 3 — Word Problems

Study this section the next time your assignment involves word problems. Word problems show up at almost all levels of math. You can be almost certain of getting some every year, so it is worth your while to learn how to deal with them. Word problems are a high-level mix requiring verbal, thinking, and computation skills. A deficiency in any or all of the three skill areas can cause difficulties, so it is no wonder that word problems tend to strike terror in the hearts of many students.

Word problems aren't all set up for you the way "normal" problems are. Before you can start computing, you have to understand a verbal description of the mathematical relationships in the problem. Then you have to turn these relationships into math symbols. Following the step-by-step sequence described below will give you a structure for dealing with word problems and make the task seem less like a hopeless jungle. We will use the problem below to "walk through" the process.

> Beth has 120 feet of fencing, all of which she will use to keep animals out of her rectangular vegetable garden. The length of the garden is twice the width. What are the dimensions of the garden?

Step 1 - First reading
Read the problem to get a general idea of what it is all about. Look up any words you do not know the precise meaning of in the index of your textbook or in a dictionary before going on to the second reading. For instance, are you sure about the meaning of the word "dimensions?"

Step 2 - Second, in-depth reading
Read the problem again slowly, this time aloud. Reading aloud adds the listening component, and slows you down; both of these factors are a big aid in understanding difficult material. The purpose of this reading is to find out 1) what the problem is asking you and 2) what information it gives

MATHEMATICS

you to work with.

The answer to question 1) is, the length and the width of the garden. The answer to question 2) is, that the fencing, which is to go all around the perimeter of the garden is 120 feet; and that the length is twice the width.

Step 3 - Translate
Take the information the problem gives you and translate it from words into math symbols. Just like translating from one language to another, you may have to change the order of the words. For example, if you are working with variables, let X equal the variable about which you know **the least**. The translation into math symbols should look something like this: **Information given**: P=120ft., X=width, 2X=length; **Find**: width and length.

Step 4 - Draw
If at all possible, make a drawing of the problem, labeling it with the information given. This step helps you to "connect" with the problem by making the physical properties described more concrete in your mind. That in turn makes the actual setting up of the problem easier.

DRAWING

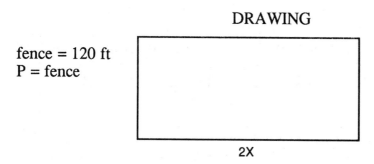

fence = 120 ft
P = fence

2X

Step 5 - Set up problem
Set up the problem for computation using math symbols. Write super clearly, to eliminate that source of mistakes.

P=2L+2W

Step 6 - Solve
Carry out the operations slowly and carefully.

120=2(2X)+2(X)
120=4X+2X
120=6X

6X=120
X=20ft=width
2X=40ft.=length

Step 7 - Judge if answer makes sense

Reread the original problem to make sure that your answer makes sense (for example, no one bats more than 1000) and that you have actually answered the question in the measurements required. For example, the answer to our sample problem is in feet, which is correct. The problem asks us to find **the dimensions**, which means the length and the width, so we were not done until we have found both of these measurements. We should also plug our figures into the formula to make sure we did not make a careless mistake.

P=2L+2W
120=2(40)+2(20)
120=80+40
120=120

The problem checks out. If your answer was not correct, find your mistake and correct it.

Practice the steps in solving word problems listed below on your next word problem assignment and you will find that proceeding according to a step-by-step plan makes word problems much less mysterious.

Step 1 - Read the problem to find out what it is all about.
Step 2 - Read the problem aloud to discover what you are to find out and the information you have to work with.
Step 3 - Translate the words into math symbols.
Step 4 - Make a drawing and label it.
Step 5 - Set up the problem using math symbols.
Step 6 - Carry out operations.
Step 7 - Check and, if needed, correct the answer.

Part 4 — Geometry

❑ As in any homework assignment, check your assignment sheet to make sure you are doing the correct pages and take note of any additional instructions or explanation the teacher gave in class. Then proceed through the following steps.◆

MATHEMATICS

Step 1 - **Study textbook and make definition cards.**

Study the textbook explanation using the system explained in Part 1 (pp. 31–33). Rushing in to do the assigned problems without first studying the textbook, makes your life more difficult than it needs to be and throws away all the helps that are built into a modern do-it-yourself geometry textbook.

Make sure to review the 3x5 definition card for any geometry definition mentioned in the textbook explanation introduced earlier in the book. This takes only a minute, but helps to anchor the definition firmly in your mind as you study the textbook explanation of the new lesson. Remember, math definitions are to the mathematician what scalpels are to the surgeon: the tools of the trade, so a student using a half-understood definition is like a surgeon operating with a dull knife.

Then fill out a 3x5 definition card for any new geometry definitions that are introduced in this lesson. (Review page 32 for instruction on how to make definition cards.) As you saw before, these cards give you an easy way to refresh your memory the next time the definition is used. The physical act of writing and making a drawing also focuses your attention on the term and gives you stronger mental input, which helps you to understand and remember each new geometry definition.

You can heighten the effect even more by saying the words aloud to yourself softly as you write them. The more thoroughly you learn these definitions the less review you need the next time they are used and the more use you get out of what you have learned.

Step 2 - **Make theorem cards.**

Use 3x5 cards for this, too. Making theorem cards takes a little time, but it helps you to learn each new theorem as it is introduced, and gives you a handy record of all the theorems you have learned. In geometry, there are usually several ways to do each proof, all of which are correct. However, the more complete your knowledge of the theorems and definitions is, the more options you have to choose from in doing proofs. This means that you are more likely to find a way to do the proof quickly, and will not encounter the terrible frustration of not having the slightest idea of how to even start the proof. You may even be able to do it with fewer steps. Theorems and definitions are very powerful time and labor saving devices. They reduce frustration and let you cut corners.

As on the model below, write the subject of the theorem across the top

MATHEMATICS

of the card (for example, congruent angles), so that you can easily sort the cards according to subject. All the cards that deal with the subject at hand will now be readily available for reference when working on a new theorem. Use abbreviations and symbols for this, such as Suppl. Copy the complete wording of the theorem underneath the subject.

Now, on the back of the card write the subject of the theorem on the top line. Make a drawing of the figure involved in the theorem. Do this carefully, so that the relationships will be clear and accurate. Write in the clues, "ifs" that you should see when working with this theorem. Draw a line under the "ifs" and fill in the "then," or conclusion, in red.

The goal in making the theorem card is to help you fully understand and remember the theorem. You are trying to get instant recall of the drawing, the idea behind the theorem, and finally the statement of the theorem in that order.

SAMPLE THEOREM CARD
front

SSAC

 Angles supplementary to the same angle are
 congruent.

SAMPLE THEOREM CARD
back

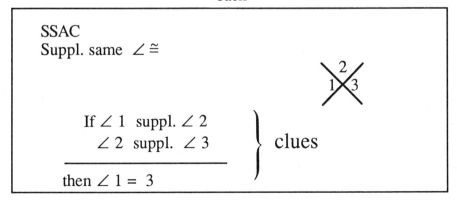

Put the theorem card with the others on the same topic in the "reference library" in front of you. You should be thoroughly familiar with the new theorem at this point and ready to proceed to the proofs that have been assigned as homework.

Step 3 - **Do homework proofs using routine below.**

1) Read the problem through first to get the general idea. Then look through your definition cards to get the exact meaning of any terms you aren't sure of. You **must** know **all** the words, because their definitions are used as reasons in the proof.

2) Read the problem over again carefully to discover the givens and what you are to prove.

3) Study the diagram in the book and identify its parts. You should be looking especially for:

- special kinds of ∡s. What kinds of ∡s have you studied lately? The ones you have just studied are very likely to "reappear."

- congruent ∡s. They are almost always part of a proof, because their parts give you a way to generate lots of new data with which to work .

- special kinds of lines, especially parallel lines. If you have them, you also have lots of congruent ∡s. Intersecting lines give you vertical, right and supplementary ∡s.

4) On the front of your paper carefully draw the figure on your homework paper using the correct proportions. Mark the givens in red. The back of your paper is reserved for writing the correct version in class of any problems you missed on the homework. This way you will have a correct version of all the proofs you had for homework to use during reviews.

Even if you can mark in the book, make your own drawing. This action makes you attend to the details of the diagram, which is precisely what you need to do. If you softly describe to yourself what you are drawing, you give yourself oral as well as visual input. This further improves your concentration and the amount of learning you get out of the time you spend.

5) Draw the lines for statements and reasons, and put down the givens. Then figure out your strategy: what theorems you will need to connect the givens to what you have to prove, since a proof is nothing but a series of connected statements.

The "then" in step 1 should match with the "if" in step 2 and so on. The tough part is to choose, from all the theorems with the "if" you are working on, the one which moves you towards your goal: what you are to prove. This is where the theorem cards you made out can come in handy. Pull all the cards that have the "if" you are working on as the conclusion you have written in red. Use trial and error as you experiment with the cards. This saves you a lot of extra writing.

Super geometry students go through the theorems they know in their heads to find the ones they need to do a particular proof. But until you get to be a super geometry student, it is easier to use the theorem cards as "crib sheets" to remind yourself of the theorems you have at your disposal. You can put the cards in the order in which you will use them, making a kind of outline, before you commit your ideas to your homework paper.

Step 4 - **Review new theorem(s).**
The last step in doing your geometry homework is to take the new theorem you have just learned and etch it into your memory with review. On a piece of scrap paper, see if you can reproduce the theorem card from memory: wording, diagram, the clues that are the "ifs," and the conclusion, the "then," marked in red. Check your work against the theorem card for accuracy and make any corrections necessary.

Below is a review of the steps you should use in doing your geometry homework.

Step 1 - Study textbook explanation and make definition cards.
Step 2 - Make theorem cards.
Step 3 - Do homework proofs.
Step 4 - Review new theorem.

Class Work

Classwork in algebra and geometry consists mostly of going over homework and introducing new material. Why bother paying attention?

The do-it-yourself format of the modern textbooks might let you get by without teacher explanation and help, but that is the hard and less efficient way to do it. A textbook can not interact with you and answer your specific questions. In addition, any background your teacher provides makes it that much easier for you to study the textbook.

Paying attention in class is one of the most useful ways to learn and remember the most material in the shortest amount of time and with the least amount of effort. Do not throw away this golden opportunity! Class work is the second part of the good math student's "secret" to good grades. You have spent a lot of time and energy understanding the homework, now you are all set to participate fully in class, and you will find that math class is much more interesting and easier to stay involved in now that you know what is going on.

Class participation is a great way to "recycle" your learning. You get a chance to see if you have really understood the homework, to get your questions answered, and have a review, all without spending a minute of "your own time."

Students have to change from one subject to another with very little time in between, so in order to get the most learning out of your math class, you need to "get into math" as quickly as possible. ❑ If you have a minute before class, read over the new theorem and/or definition card you made during the homework. That should get your mind off the last subject and onto math in a hurry. ◆

The next thing is to stay involved. A good way to do that, is through 100% participation: ❑ Answer mentally when other students are called on, rather than turning off.◆ The more you mentally process what you have learned, the easier it is to remember.

Another way of staying involved is to do a really good job correcting your homework. While it is much more fun to concentrate on the problems you did correctly when the teacher goes over the homework, your main concern during the homework correction process should be with any problems that you missed. As the teacher goes over each problem, write the correct version of any problem that you missed on the back of your paper. The purpose of the maneuver is to provide yourself with good reference material for review.

Make sure that you understand each problem before the teacher finishes with it. That way you will avoid making the same mistakes over and over again. If you have any questions, get them answered when the teacher goes over the problem. Do not wait until twenty minutes later to get up your courage to ask a question. When you ask a question that does not pertain to the work at hand, it breaks the flow of the lesson, and the teacher will be annoyed rather than pleased.

The second part of your task in class is to get a head start on the next day's homework. ❑ You need to **write down the exact assignment** on your assignment sheet. As noted before, much student time is wasted doing the wrong assignment. Don't let that happen to you.◆

In addition, pay careful attention to any pre-teaching of the assignment. ❑ Write down any special directions or sample problems your teacher provides either directly on your assignment sheet or on a separate sheet of paper you keep in your notebook along with your math homework. Think along while the teacher is explaining, and get any questions you have answered. Attention now will save you a lot of time and effort when you do your homework. ◆

Good class work, then, has three functions: 1) to prepare well for the homework assigned for the next night, 2) to check and correct your understanding of the homework done the night before, and 3) to reinforce your learning, so that you will be able to remember the material for the test. If you do your part, you will also impress the teacher that you are a serious math student, and help the teacher to help you get the most out of the course.

Studying for Tests

Why in the world should a student worry about reviewing if a test has not even been announced yet? You have lots of things to do that seem more pressing. Researchers have discovered that the usual way of doing things (finishing the homework and then forgetting about it until a test looms) **is the most inefficient way** to go about learning — you forget almost all of the material you have worked on. Regular, spaced review can change that into remembering almost everything (Thomas and Robinson, p. 185.)

However, you do not get something for nothing. The price for this high reward is to review at times when there is no threat of a test: right after you are done with the homework, just before class, and as a regular part of your class work. If you do that, your review before tests should be fairly easy and you'll more than win back the time you invested in earlier reviews. Math students have an additional incentive to review regularly: the cumulative nature of mathematics. The more thoroughly you know past and present material, the easier it is to master new material — you will not be playing "catch up" all the time.

Like all other aspects of becoming a good math student, there are ways to go about it which give you the maximum learning (and therefore better grades) for the time you invest. The goal of your efforts is to give yourself the best possible chance of doing well on the test. **Being prepared for tests is *essential* for good test grades.** Good test grades in turn are the basic ingredient to good grades in math as they are in your other courses. Follow the steps below and you should come to the test well prepared.

Step 1 - Note the test in your assignment book.
❑ When your teacher announces a test, write "test chapter -" in red, so that you cannot overlook it, on your assignment sheet under the date for which the test is scheduled . This sounds obvious, but students sometimes do not do this right away, and then forget to enter the test date at a later time. The result is that you may forget to study and do poorly on the test.◆

❑ Then mark the two days before the test "study for test chapter -." Do not schedule just one night to study for a test. Two shorter sessions will get you further than one long one, and if you have any problems the first night, you'll have a chance to get help the next day.◆

Step 2 - Find out what you do not know.
On the first day that you have scheduled to study for the test, check your assignment sheet to be sure that you are studying the correct material. Spend an hour and a half getting as far as you can through the rest of the study program. Whatever is not done on day one, is your job for day two.

"Get into" studying for the test by quizzing yourself on the definition cards that you made out when you did the homework for the chapter or unit on which you are having the test. Look at the term on the front of the card and say the definition to yourself, make the drawing, and write down the non-example you thought of. Then turn the card over and check to see if you were correct. Definitions that were 100% correct, go into the **know** pile, the rest go into the **don't know** pile.

Geometry students should test themselves on the theorem cards by looking at the front of each card and trying to reproduce what is on the back. Only study those theorems relating to the material that will be on the test. Theorems you know go into the **know** pile, the others into the **don't know** pile. If you have done a good job on the homework and classwork, almost all the definition and theorem cards are probably in the **know** pile.

Now take your textbook's chapter or unit review test. This will help you to sort out what you remember and what you need to relearn. Correct your work, marking the problems or proofs you got wrong with a big red X. Rewrite these on another sheet of paper. This will be the test to take after you have studied the items you missed.

Step 3 - **Study the material you need to relearn**.
You need spend no more time on what you already know. The definition and theorem cards in the **don't know** piles as well as the rewritten problems and proofs cover the material you should concentrate on now.

Rewrite each definition and back of theorem card in the **don't know** pile, reciting each word to yourself as you write it; quiz yourself again. Each time you go through the cycle, there should be fewer cards in the **don't know** pile. Do this for no more than a half hour. Any cards remaining in a **don't know** pile after that should be clipped onto a 4x6 card labeled **difficult cases**. (This card is discussed below.)

Now you are ready to work on the problems you need to relearn. Find the place in the textbook where each problem or proof that you missed during Step 2 is covered. Reread the textbook explanation, and do the sample problems. Then find the homework you did on this material and redo the items that you had trouble with when you did the original homework. They should be all ready and waiting for you on the back of the homework. If you have kept all your homework papers in order and labeled them well, the proper problems or proofs should be easy to find.

It would be a good idea to get at least this far on the first day you study for the test. This gives you an opportunity to ask your teacher in class the next day to explain anything that you do not clearly understand at this point. Listen super carefully if there is an in-class review. Your teacher has probably already made up the test and wants everyone to do well on it, so items mentioned during in-class review will almost certainly be on the test.

On a clean sheet of paper labeled "items missed during in-class review" write down any problems, theorems, or definitions you did not know during the review. These are the first items you should "hit" on your second and last study day. **The probability that these problems** (most likely with different numbers) **will show up on the test is very high.**

"Pulling an all nighter" studying for a test is not a good idea. And you will not even have to contemplate such a thing, because you have prepared systematically and thoroughly. This gives you the rare luxury of using the second day of study to just put the finishing touches on your review for the test. You do not have to make up the learning that should have taken place during homework, classwork, and the in-class review.

Start your last day of review with the "items missed during in-class review." If all went according to plan, there are not even very many such items. Look up how to do each of these problems, and redo problems like each of the missed items. (There should be other examples of the same variety of problem in both the Chapter Review Test and your homework.) If any of the items you missed of the in-class review were theorems or definitions, pull the relevant cards out of your pile and relearn the theorems or definitions.

Continue your program of studying for the test where you left off the night before. Then just to be extra sure that you are 100% prepared for the test, do the problems or proofs that you missed when you took the chapter or unit review test. Again mark any items missed with a big red X. These are the **difficult cases**, but there will be very few of these if you have done a good job. ❏ Write these problems on a 4x6 card so you can review them when you have a free minute or two and just before you walk in to take the test.◆ The definition and theorem cards you had trouble with should be clipped to the 4x6 card as well.

You are all set for the test. Get a sound night's sleep, and eat a good breakfast in the morning, so you will be able to do your very best on the test. Once more, briefly, the steps in studying for tests are:

Step 1 - Note the test on your assignment sheet.
Step 2 - Find out what you do not know.
Step 3 - Study the material you need to relearn.

Taking Tests

Testing in mathematics is a straight-forward affair. You get problems and theorems that are very much like those you had for homework. Usually, only the numbers and letters are different. There are no essay questions. (The definition of specialized terms is about the only writing you are asked to do.) Multiple choice and matching questions are rare. To an extent that is true in no other class, you get on the test what you have practiced on homework and in class.

The grade you receive in math courses is largely based on your quiz and test scores, so getting the best possible grades on tests is a must. The general principles of good test-taking were discussed in Chapter I (pp. 20–23), and will be applied here to your math course.

There are two important ingredients to getting good test grades in any subject: 1) knowing the material and 2) good test-taking techniques. Good test-taking cannot overcome not knowing the material, but it can help you get maximum credit for what you do know.

If you followed the suggestions presented in this chapter, then you have thoroughly learned the material that will be on the test. Your task now is to set up the best possible conditions for taking the test; give yourself all the breaks you can. The object is to achieve a calm, cool, confident frame of mind that is so helpful in getting good test grades. ❑ Make it to class in plenty of time with all the materials you will need and nothing else.◆ Then follow the steps below.

Step 1 - ❑ **Read all directions carefully.**◆

Step 2 - **Do easy problems.**
Showing each step clearly, work on all the problems or proofs you can do easily. When you show all the steps, you not only reduce the chances of getting lost, but you might also get partial credit for otherwise incorrect answers.
❑ Work in a steady, unhurried, but purposeful manner. Do not stop to ponder items that you are not sure of. Go as far in each problem or proof as you can. Put a check mark in front of any problem or proof that you have not completed, so you can find it again easily and go on. The object is to get all the easy credit you can before you go back and spend time doing the items that presented difficulty. Do not spend unnecessary time on any one problem.◆

After you finish each problem or proof, remember your good habits from the homework and check your answer. Does the answer make sense? Can you find any careless mistakes? If you are working on an equation, plug your answer(s) in for the unknown(s) and see if the problem works out correctly. If not, go back and find your error. Why spend precious test time going over what you have already done? A minute or two spent checking your answers should save you from careless mistakes, and people who want to get the highest possible grades on tests cannot afford to make careless mistakes!

Step 3 - Do word problems.

If there are word problems to do, follow exactly the same procedure you used when such problems were assigned for homework (pp. 37–39). Leave word problems until you have gone through the test once and done all the easy problems, because word problems require a bit of time. Just be sure to leave plenty of space for them when you go through the test the first time.

Step 4 - Do checked problems.

After you finish the word problems (if any), go back and work on the problems or proofs you checked. Below is a summary of the steps to follow in applying good test-taking to math tests:

Step 1 - Read all directions carefully.
Step 2 - Do easy problems.
Step 3 - Do word problems.
Step 4 - Do checked problems.

Conclusion

You have now learned how to adapt the general rules for being a good student to the subject of mathematics, which is **the** most exact subject you have in school. Every single word you read counts; no word can be skipped.

This chapter devoted the most space to showing you how to do the homework in algebra and geometry as well as how to do word problems, and you, too, should spend the most time and effort on this bottom level of the pyramid to good grades in math.

When you do a thorough job on the homework, you are well prepared for the next level: class work. Here you need to participate fully, and write the correct version of any problems or proofs that were not correct on the homework. You should also write down the new assignment and any help your teacher gives you on the new homework.

The cumulative nature of mathematics makes the review level (right after you finish your homework in math, just before class, during class, and before tests) an especially important one in math. The "pay-off" for each hour invested in review is fantastic. This chapter presented steps to help you structure your reviews, so that you will be fully prepared at test time.

The final level, taking tests, showed you how to get the most credit for the learning you have accumulated. This is important, since tests are the biggest part of your math grade. Spend the time applying the suggestions in this chapter to your math course conscientiously, and watch your grades improve.

REFERENCES

Baldridge, Kenneth P. *Baldridge Reading Instruction Materials.* Greenwich, CT: 1977.

Pauk, Walter. *How to Study in College.* 2nd ed. Boston: Houghton Mifflin, 1974.

Pauk, Walter. *Successful Scholarship.* Englewood Cliffs, NJ.: Prentice-Hall, 1966.

Thomas, Ellen Lamar and Robinson, H. Alan. *Improving Reading in Every Class.* 3rd. ed. Boston: Allyn & Bacon, 1982.

Tobias, Sheila. "Insiders and Outsiders." *Academic Connections.* Winter, 1988.

Tobias, Sheila. *Succeed with Math: Every Student's Guide to Conquering Math Anxiety.* New York: College Entrance Examination

CHAPTER III
SCIENCE

LITTLE THINGS THAT HELP

1. Get familiar with the subject matter and vocabulary of science out of school.
    a. Read the science section of the daily newspaper.
    b. Read articles on science in popular magazines.
    c. Watch science shows on TV like Nova, National Geographic, Discover.
2. Get into the right mind set for science: expect reading the science textbook (like math) to take up to ten times longer than reading a novel and allow enough time.
3. Write out points you did not understand in your homework to get clarification in class the next day.
4. Preview chapter before reading to get basic structure and ideas.
5. Write bold print terms and definitions on 3x5 cards as part of prereading of the textbook.
6. Make full use of all helps (such as a glossary of terms) available in the textbook.

Tasks, Difficulties, and Advantages in Studying Science

Many students think science, like mathematics, is a particularly "scary" and difficult subject, and that becoming a good science student requires a whole new brain. This is not true; as in other subjects, what is necessary is to learn certain skills and methods for applying them. In this chapter you will learn to read and write like a scientist, to follow a lecture, and to do laboratory work.

In many ways science is closely related to mathematics, so it is not surprising that scientists use language a lot like mathematicians do. The "scientific method," requires that scientists (and students of science) be very exact in their observations and in formulating the conclusions that are based on these observations. The reason scientists do this is so that their experiments can be reproduced — the technical term is "replicated" — by other scientists and the conclusions compared exactly. To make this possible, scientists, like mathematicians, use words and formulas with one and only one meaning that can be clearly understood by other scientists all over the world. For example, to a chemist the abbreviation "Ag" always stands for the element "silver"; it does not mean "agriculture" or "against" or anything else.

Way back in the beginnings of science, scientists really did have a universal language. All scholars understood Latin. Nowadays few scientists can write or speak in Latin, but it is hardly surprising that many of the words used in science still show their Latin origins. To the modern student, long, scientific words look difficult. But they really are not. These "Latinized" terms are actually easier to read than a lot of "normal" English words if you break these long words down into syllables, and apply the phonetic rules. They are likely to be pronounced exactly as they are spelled.

The writing style of scientists, too, is very much like that of the mathematicians. In other words, science writing is "fact-oriented," non-emotional and compact. You do not have to "read between the lines" in science to get at the author's "real" meaning. In fact, science writing tends to be almost a form of shorthand. For example, formulas or symbols often take the place of long-winded explanations. As a result, slow, precise reading is a must.

In addition, class work may present a communication problem. Science teachers often use the lecture method of teaching to present the material, with the teacher doing almost all of the talking. This may be your first contact with this method of teaching and like all new things, it takes a little getting used to.

Lectures are usually presented either as an introduction to new material or as further explanation of what has already been assigned in the textbook. In either case, there is an interaction between the homework and the lecture. If the lecture is an introduction to new material, the more you concentrate and get out of the lecture, the easier the night's homework will be. If the lecture explains more about textbook material previously covered as homework, the teacher builds the lecture on the assumption that you have done the homework and are therefore familiar with the topic. You will be lost in class the next day, if you have not studied the assignment carefully.

Your science course may also be your first experience with lab work. This is your introduction to the "scientific method": experimentation and exact observation. It is absolutely necessary that you read and follow directions extra carefully, observe the experiments precisely, and write down the results exactly, or your conclusions will be wrong! A hit-or-miss approach to lab procedures almost guarantees disaster. On the other hand, practical types should enjoy this hands-on part of science; you get to work with concrete objects.

The study of science is not just a minefield of problems, you have some big advantages as well. You will be able to apply your knowledge of science to many of your everyday experiences, and you will notice what a big part of modern life science is. There is an abundance of easy-to-understand science material available in the form of TV programs, articles in popular magazines and even your daily newspaper. Watching science programs and reading science articles is a relatively painless way to familiarize yourself with the vocabulary and theories of the subject. If you use these resources, you will find it much easier to read, listen to, understand, and remember what you learn in your science course.

If you want to be really smart about this, you might study the table of contents of your textbook to find out what topics you will be studying during the year. Then watch for programs and articles on these topics. Make a habit of checking the TV program guide every week and look through the daily newspapers for appropriate science articles.

As usual, the levels of the Pyramid to Good Grades (next page) form the bold print subdivisions of the chapter. And, again, the easiest way to proceed is to do a good job on each step in turn, but you should concentrate most of your time on homework, and spend increasingly less time as you move up the levels of the pyramid.

Pyramid to Good Grades in Science

Taking Tests

Read directions carefully. Read objective questions carefully. Answer questions you know right away. Answer essay questions. Answer difficult objective questions.

Studying for Tests

Note date. Review end of chapter questions, textbook graphics, lab summaries, 3x5 cards. In-class review and "don't know" 3x5 cards.

Class Work

Labs: review procedure, collect materials, follow directions step-by-step, write results, write lab summary. Lectures: review 3x5 cards, ask and answer questions, take notes.

Homework

Preread assignment in textbook, make bold print vocabulary cards, read textbook, take notes, memorize terms, formulas, etc., prepare for next day lab.

Homework

This is the most important level on the pyramid to success as a science student. Although you may get few pop quizzes and the regular tests seem a long way off, put the most time and effort into your homework. Doing a good job at this stage will increase your attention in class, and make it easier for you to remember the material for the inevitable test. At first you may have to pressure yourself to do the homework well, but that will not be difficult, once you see how much easier your life is when you follow the suggestions in this chapter.

Before discussing the steps to go through in doing your home work, a discussion of how to read those long, unfamiliar words and a method of adjusting your reading to scientific writing (the "back-and-forth" system) is in order.

How to Read Those Long Words

Reading the textbook and lab procedures is the most important part of doing your homework in science courses. Your goal is to understand and learn what is contained in these materials. Unfamiliar words are the main stumbling blocks to reading, understanding, and remembering science materials. Actually, as I said earlier, they are nothing to be afraid of.

Strategy 1: **Concentrate on bold print words.**
If the word you are having trouble with is one of the words in **bold** print, you are in luck. **Bold** print words signify important concepts in the chapter that the author thinks you will not know. These concepts are explained either right before or right after the first appearance of the word. Also, these same bold print words will be in the glossary at the end of your textbook. Keep a book mark at the beginning of the glossary so you can refer to it easily. Because you will be making cards for these terms anyway, they will not be a problem. If you have the meaning, go on to *Strategy 4.*

Other unfamiliar words may not be in bold print in the chapter you are studying. Check the glossary anyway; they may be there after all, because they were introduced earlier. If not, resist the impulse to just skip them. They are often not as tricky as they might appear at first glance. If you follow the system described below for reading these words, science books will not be so baffling and mysterious.

First of all, get yourself "psyched" for the project of unlocking those long, strange-looking, scientific words by looking upon the task as a challenge. Apply your thinking powers and what you already know about words to this word you do not know — like a detective solving a mystery. In fact, that is not a bad comparison. Just as in mystery stories, the information you need to solve the mystery is probably right under your nose. You just do not yet recognize it.

Strategy 2:: **Recognize a "word within a word" – prefixes, suffixes, root words, and endings.**

The big piece of "hidden" information about scientific words that you need to know to unlock these words is the system scientists use to build new words in the first place. What they do is tack an old, familiar suffix (back of the word) or prefix (front of the word) onto an old, familiar Latin or English root word. Scientists use these prefixes, suffixes, and root words just like "Lego blocks," putting them in various combinations to make new words that are easy for scientists to remember and figure out because they already know the meaning of the parts. When you figure out and learn what the parts mean, you, too, will find scientific words easy to understand and remember.

We will use the word <u>oceanographer</u> to show you how to go about unlocking such a word. In this case the suffix <u>ographer</u> was tacked onto the familiar English word <u>ocean</u>. In working with long, complicated words, just as in other aspects of learning, you want to make your life as easy as possible. Follow the familiar strategy of working from what you know to figure out what you do not yet know. Take a good look at our word. If you have recognized the word <u>ocean</u> as a "word within a word," you know that whatever it is, it has something to do with oceans. You already have a big part of the puzzle figured out — for "free," so to speak.

The next part of our mystery-solving operation is to figure out what the suffix <u>ographer</u> means. Try to think of other words, whose meaning you do know, that use the same suffix. The word <u>geographer</u> comes to mind. Now use your knowledge of English words. Both <u>oceanographer</u> and <u>geographer</u> have the familiar English ending <u>er</u>. If you cannot remember what this ending means, again think of words you do know with that same ending. <u>Farmer</u>, <u>teacher</u>, <u>baker</u>, and so forth are ordinary English words with that ending. You know it means "one who does something" and the something he or she does comes right before the ending. So, both an <u>oceanographer</u> and a <u>geographer</u> must be people who do something, And what they do must be in the <u>ograph</u> part of the word.

SCIENCE

Now, we happen to know, that a <u>geographer</u> studies or writes about the earth. If you cannot remember the meaning of any similar word, you have to look up your word in the dictionary at this point, but next time you come across a word ending in <u>ographer</u>, you will be able to use this system.

Putting all the bits and pieces of our "language smarts" together in the same "Lego block" system the scientists use, we discover, that we actually knew more than we thought about the word. In fact, we have got the meaning:

<u>ocean</u> – deep, salty water

<u>ograph</u> – to write about or study

<u>er</u> – one who does something

So, that is what the word means: a person who writes about or studies oceans.

Now comes the big payoff. Knowing that scientists will use the "Lego block" system of word-building whenever they can, you have just given yourself the key to unlocking a whole batch of sophisticated words, such as:

lexic<u>ographer</u>

cart<u>ographer</u>

bi<u>ographer</u>

orth<u>ographer</u>

The next time you come across a word with the suffix <u>ographer</u>, you will not have to start from scratch in figuring out the word. You will know a big chunk of it already, because you went to the trouble this time of figuring out that a word ending in <u>ographer</u> will mean "someone who writes about or studies something" and the something they write about or study comes right before the suffix <u>ographer</u>.

This means that **you can improve your comprehension of scientific words quickly and dramatically**. Each time you spend the time and effort to learn the meaning of one of those "Lego block" word parts, you learn part of the meaning of a whole lot of words at the same time. Now, see if you can apply this system to find the meaning of the word <u>micromanipulator</u>.

Strategy 3: **Isolate the word and divide it into syllables.**

If you can see no "word within a word," or recognize any prefix, suffix, root word or ending, the next strategy to try is to isolate the problem word by writing it on a piece of scrap paper and dividing the syllables with slashes. Pronounce each syllable in turn applying the vowel rules. — Vowels (the letters a,e,i,o,u) are short unless 1) they are at the end of a syllable, 2) are followed by a consonant and an "e," or 3) there are two vowels in a row. A long vowel "says its own name." — Once you have figured out how to pronounce the syllables, all you need to do is to put the syllables back together to pronounce the whole word.

Example: in/ de/ pen/ dent

Pronouncing the word may be all it takes for you to know its meaning. If so, go on to *Strategy 4*. However, if the meaning of the word still escapes you, the next step is to look for meaning clues. Read the rest of the sentence. Very often the other words in a sentence give you the meaning of the problem word. When you think you have the meaning, go on to *Strategy 4*.

Strategy 4: **Test your meaning by rereading the sentence.**
If the sentence makes sense, chances are good that you have the correct meaning for the word. Always check your understanding of the word by seeing if it makes sense in the sentence, and **stop the process when you have the meaning.**

If none of the methods described above help you to decipher the word, you need to look the word up in the dictionary. Be sure to choose the meaning that the dictionary indicates is used in science. Again, test the correctness by rereading the sentence and making sure it makes sense.

To review, the steps in finding the meaning of long, unknown words are:
1) Check the glossary, especially for bold print words.
2) Use your "language smarts" to take the word apart and discover meaningful segments of the word.
    a) Is there a "word within a word?"
    b) Is there a familiar English ending?
    c) Is there a prefix or suffix or root word whose meaning you know?
    d) If not, are there words whose meaning you do know that use the same prefix, suffix, or root word?
3) Isolate the word.
    a) Write it on a piece of scrap paper, marking the syllables with slashes.
    b) Apply the vowel rules.
4) Read the sentence in which the word is found for context clues to its meaning.

Now practice reading a page of today's science homework. Every time you come across a troublesome word, follow the plan above. At first it will take a little time to figure out new words, but after the system becomes second nature to you, it will get to be much quicker and easier.

Read Science Textbooks like Scientist do: the Back and Forth Method

Now, on to reading the textbook. In addition to pronouncing and understanding long words, you obviously also need to be able to understand the ideas the textbook author is presenting. Scientists have developed a special way of writing, and as a student of science, you need to adjust your reading habits to this method.

Science textbooks have to be read very slowly and carefully; every word counts. The ideas are presented in a very condensed form. It can take you up to ten times as long to read science materials as it would take you to read a novel for English class. But do not get disheartened: Science assignments are much shorter than English assignments. **If you think of the task as thoughtful study, rather than "reading," you are on the right track**.

Success in reading scientific materials depends a lot on your ability to translate the words you read back into concrete objects; you need to learn to visualize what the author writes about. To help you do this, science authors include figures, diagrams, charts and pictures.

The way to get the most out of these helps is to use a "back and forth" system of reading. That is, when you see signal words like "as shown in figure ..." or "diagram ...," shift your thoughts and eyes from the text to the chart or diagram (usually on the same page) and read the caption very carefully. Do not go back to the text until you feel sure you can explain the figure, chart or diagram to someone else.

Use the "back and forth" system while studying the chart or diagram itself as well. When the caption refers to a specific feature, such as points or lines, find these in the figure before going back to the caption. You may need to go back and forth as many as six times between the figure and the caption while studying a single figure.

Practice the back and forth system on tonight's homework to get the "feel" of the method. Again, as in any new method of working, do not be surprised if it takes a little longer the first few times. But the extra time will soon "pay for itself" – when you get to class tomorrow and know what the lesson is all about.

Prereading Activities

After these general words on how to go about reading science materials, you are ready to take up the textbook. But, again, do not rush in and read the assignment first word to last. The whole process will go much quicker and you will understand more if you spend some time becoming familiar with the assignment and follow a plan for studying it.

Step 1 – **Find out the main points**.

Science textbooks, like all other textbooks, are easier to read and understand if you know how the author has organized the chapter and what the main points are going to be. The first day that you are assigned part of a chapter spend a few minutes prereading. ❏ **Read the title, the introduction, the section headings, and the conclusion**. Read the introduction with the idea, "The author is trying to indicate the highpoints of the chapter, so that I will know what is significant when I get to it." The section headings are actually the major points (the Roman numerals) from the author's own outline. In the textbook they are numbered and printed in larger letters, written in a different color, or highlighted in some other way to catch your eye and make you notice them. The paragraphs that follow, all deal with the subject indicated in the heading. Next, turn to the conclusion. This is actually a recap of the chapter. Here the author reviews the main points of the chapter.◆

Step 2 – **Make vocabulary cards**.

Now go back through the pages that you have been assigned and **make a vocabulary card for each bold print term** on one side of a 3x5 card and the definition (found either right before or right after the term) on the other. Write the terms in your favorite, bright color dividing the syllables with slashes. This makes pronouncing the word easier and gives you a stronger visual input. The mechanical act of writing even helps you learn the terms. The advantage of this procedure is that your reading and understanding of the assignment will be much easier if you already know the most important terms. In addition, the cards also make review easy. To get the most benefit out of making vocabulary cards, do it right away, so you can use your knowledge the entire time you are working on this chapter; do not wait until you are studying for the test.

Step 3 – **Make a work sheet for taking notes**.

Taking notes helps you to remember what you have read and gives you a way to review without having to reread the textbook. The idea behind making yourself a work sheet is to give you questions to look for in your reading, and to avoid having to look back for the questions. You have them right in front of you.

Use only the left side of your paper for notes on the textbook; the right side should be kept free for class notes. If you write left handed, just do the opposite: right side for homework notes and left side for class notes. In either case the idea is that the ring binder should not interfere with your writing in class. The advantage of this system is that you have much less writing to do in class: you only have to write down items that are **not** in your homework notes, making it much easier to keep up with the information presented by the teacher.

Start by writing the chapter title on the top line. If your teacher provided questions, use these, if not, use the self-check questions in the textbook. To allow plenty of room for the answers, leave at least six lines between questions, and do not hesitate to use several sheets of paper.

Practice all the prereading steps on your next science assignment, and you will find it much easier to study the chapter and remember what you have read when you get to class the next day. Below is a summary of the steps:

Step 1 – Find the main points.
Step 2 – Make vocabulary cards.
Step 3 – Make a work sheet for taking notes.

Reading and Taking Notes

With all this preparation, the actual reading and note-taking will go much faster and be more successful than you are used to. Work with one numbered section at a time. Start by reading the section through slowly using the back and forth system, and the reading hints presented above. Keeping a scratch pad on hand to make your own drawings to help you understand is a good idea too.

After reading the section through once, read the first question on your worksheet. Look for the answer in the section you just read. Write the answer in your own words in the blank space on your worksheet, and check it by rereading that part of the section that gave you the answer. Using your own words takes a little longer at this point, but it is well worth the effort, because it gives you a check on how well you understand the material: what you do not understand, you cannot state in your own words. In addition, it will also be easier to remember information you have mentally reworked.

After finishing each section go through one more step: pause a minute and mentally review the main points of what you have just read. This little step can help you remember twice as much as you would otherwise remember. (Thomas and Robinson, p.311).

❑ When you have finished all your science homework, spend a few minutes to fix the questions and answers in your mind by covering up the answers and trying to answer each question in turn from memory. Check your answer immediately after saying it. Reread the correct version in your notes of any answer you did not get right. The words do not have to be exactly the same, but you do need to be able to recap the ideas. As a final touch, quiz yourself on the vocabulary cards.◆

Memorizing

At some time in your career as a science student, you are bound to have to memorize something. (An example would be chemical formulas.) There are ways to make this task a little easier: utilize a quizzing procedure to sort out items you already know, attach meaning to the items you have to memorize whenever possible, and use a multi-sensory learning procedure.

The first step is to isolate the items you want to memorize. Write the items on the front of 3x5 cards, and what they represent on the back. (If the items were bold print terms, you have already done this part, and can go on to the quizzing procedure.) To give your brain as strong a visual message as you can, use large numbers or letters and your favorite color. Add the listening component by saying the item clearly and distinctly as you write. Then use the quizzing procedure below to see if you have learned any of the items "for free" just by making the cards.

Quizzing Procedure

❑ Look at the front of each card in turn and try to recite what is on the back. If the item is a formula or something long and complicated, write it on a sheet of scratch paper. Turn the card over, and if your version matches the card 100%, put that card in a pile labeled "**science know**." These are the items you learned "for free." If your version does not match the card, it goes into a "**science don't know**" pile. These cards need the intensive and more time-consuming treatment of the memorizing procedure.◆

Memorizing Procedure

❏ Take each of the cards in the "**don't know**" pile in turn and look first at the front. Say each item slowly and accurately five times, and concentrate hard on picturing the word in "your mind's eye" for five seconds after each time you say the item. Try to think of something to pair this item with, and spend another five seconds thinking of the two items together. (For instance, you might pair the formula for photosynthesis with your favorite food — after all, that is how plants make food.) Then turn the card over and concentrate on etching that part into your memory.

To find out which cards can be switched from the "**don't know**" to the "**know**" pile repeat the quizzing procedure above with these cards after you have gone through the memorizing procedure. Your "**don't know**" pile should be a good deal smaller now. It would be nice to keep recycling this procedure until your entire "**don't know**" pile has disappeared, but stopping when you know three fourths of the cards is more efficient. You will go through the memorizing and quizzing procedures with this group, the hard-core cases, again when you review.◆

Lab Procedures — You have to do Everything Right Every Time

Laboratory experiments are when you get to act like a scientist. This is the fun part of science, but getting accurate results from an experiment requires performing the steps in the **precise** order written in the lab procedure, making **exact measurements**, observing carefully, and writing the results up precisely. Almost right is wrong! You can see how closely mathematics and science are related. Math is the only other course that requires such exactitude.

An added problem is that you usually do not have unlimited time to perform the experiments. For most experiments, if you do not finish the lab in time, you will have to start all over during a make-up period. Time pressure makes most people nervous, and when you are nervous you are likely to make mistakes.

One way to cut down on time-related mistakes, especially if you are a slow reader or have trouble following directions exactly, is to study the lab procedure the night before. That way, when you get to the experiment itself, you will already know what you have to do. You can be calm, cool, and collected and work at the steady but unhurried pace which leads to doing experiments well and finishing them in time.

The steps below (adapted from Thomas and Robinson, pp. 318-321) provide a good system for doing this.

Step 1 – Preread to get general idea of the lab and remove roadblocks of unknown words.

All difficult reading is easier if you find out what the material is about in general before you read for detailed information. In this case, read the title of the lab and the introduction to find out the purpose of the experiment, the supplies you will need, and how each piece of equipment fits into doing the experiment. If you come across a word you do not know, underline it and read on. When you have finished your first reading of the lab, Finally, go back and read the underlined words using the system, described on pp. 57–61, that you use for reading unknown words in your textbook. Even one word you do not know can ruin an experiment, so do not try to save time at this point.

Next, pick out the bold print terms you do not already have on 3x5 cards and make cards for them. These are the "official words" for that particular experiment and it is absolutely essential that you can pronounce them and know precisely what they mean. If the lab procedure itself does not make the term clear enough get the definition to write on the back of the card from the glossary of your textbook.

Step 2 – Read with thoroughness.

Now read the detailed procedure slowly and carefully, with the same back-and-forth technique you used in studying your textbook assignments (pp. 61–62). Be sure to give pictures and diagrams careful attention. Pictures and diagrams are very important in lab procedures, because they show you very clearly what you are to do.

As you read, use yellow highlighter to mark any cautions or warnings. (Heeding such warnings as "put stoppers on the tubes only after all seven have been prepared," saves you from committing serious errors.) At the same time take a red magic marker and draw a box around all measurements to make them stick out. These have to be 100% accurate.

SCIENCE

Fifty seconds means precisely fifty seconds as measured by a stop watch or second hand, not fifty-one or forty-nine. Stop and think or reread whenever you need to. The object is to understand the directions 100%.

Step 3 — **Quickly reread lab procedure to get sense of the whole procedure again**.

The purpose of this is to concentrate on the whole after you concentrated on the parts. If you have any questions in your mind at this point, write them on a sheet of paper and ask your teacher to clear them up **before lab begins**. You are all set and ready to carry out your experiment successfully the next day.

Follow this plan to study you lab procedure the night **before** your next lab. It will probably take you an hour but your performance in lab the next day will make it an hour well spent. You will know what you are doing. If you do not study the procedures ahead of time, you have to do everything during the lab time: study the instructions **and** do the experiment.

In addition, knowing what to expect at each step means that if an error did occur, you would be able to catch it, correct it, and go on. No big deal. The results would not cripple your lab. However, if you did not prepare ahead of time, it is practically certain that you will become pressured and confused. As a result, you will not correct mistakes in time, have to start over, and maybe not finish at all. Chaos, confusion, and frustration all around. "It's a bad scene."

Just to fix it in your mind, below is a summary of the method for studying labs procedures:

Step 1 – **Prereading**
    a– Read title and introduction.
    b– Put bold print terms on cards.
    c– Read the rest of the lab quickly underlining difficult words.
    d– Read difficult words using the system on pp. 57–60.
Step 2 – **Thorough Reading**
    a– Carefully read detailed procedure.
    b– Highlight warnings and cautions in yellow.
    c– Frame measurements in red.
Step 3 – **Quick Rereading of Whole Lab Procedure**

Class Work

Class work in science consists mostly of labs and lectures. Since we have just been talking about how to prepare for lab the night before, we will take care of lab first.

Lab

To begin with, you can be confident that you can do your work calmly and coolly, because you are on time, equipped with the materials you have prepared. This is how it should be: you can be an efficient scientist during the lab, because you have studied the lab the night before. Punctuality and preparation will put you in the frame of mind that is likely to lead to accurate procedures, measurements, and observations — just what you need to do the experiment successfully in the limited time that is given.

In the five minutes while the lab is coming to order, work at setting up optimal working conditions for yourself. Ask the teacher to clear up any questions you had while studying the lab the night before. Look over the highlighted cautions and warnings, the measurements framed in red, and any illustrations of how you are to set things up. As we said earlier, timing and accuracy in measurement and reporting are the watchwords during labs. Here are some further tips to help you proceed even more efficiently through lab:

1) Collect all your materials **before** you start. When you have placed an item listed in your lab procedure on your table put a penciled check mark in front of the item. This way you do not have to reread the list of materials again and again, and when all items are checked off, you can be sure that you have everything you need.

2) Mark your place in the directions by putting a marker (4x6 card or sheet of paper) under the line of instructions you are currently following. This keeps your place, and you will not waste time rereading what you have already done, or, worse, accidentally skipping a step. As you proceed with the experiment, move the marker down accordingly.

3) As soon as you get a result in the course of the experiment, measure it exactly and write it in the proper place on the chart or table in your lab procedure. Do not wait until the end of the whole experiment, because you are likely to forget the precise results.

If you follow this system, the next step, writing up your lab report, will be easy. You can draw the correct conclusions, because you will know what the experiment was designed to show you, and what actually happened while you were performing the experiment.

If you are not required to write a formal lab report, write a summary anyway as soon as you can after the end of the lab to remind yourself what the lab was all about. You will need this for review. These can be rough notes, without perfect sentences, but do include the following information: the question the experiment was designed to answer, the results, and the conclusions that can be drawn from the results.

Writing Laboratory Reports

To begin with, one word of warning: Write the rough draft of your lab report as soon as possible after the end of the lab when the work is still fresh in your mind. If you wait until the next day, it will take twice as long to achieve the same results, four times as long if you wait until the following week. Then the night before the report is due, you only have to polish up your writing to actually hand in a second and not a first draft. That should help you get a good grade on your lab reports.

A lab report is a formal way of writing up your findings in a particular experiment or series of experiments. Such reports should be written in "scientific style": clear, concise, with all the information that is necessary so that someone else could perform the same experiment and compare his or her results to yours.

Teachers differ greatly in what they want the finished lab to be like, so before starting to write a lab report, it is essential to find out exactly what information your teacher wants you to include. The teacher should also indicate whether the report is to be written with a reader in mind who knows nothing about the experiment, or for someone who knows the basic scientific problem, but not the results you obtained. For good grades on lab reports, follow your teacher's instructions precisely, and do not be afraid to ask questions.

Use your lab reports to practice presenting material in the complete, but compressed style that scientists use, providing all the required information, and only the required information. Make your own work easier and more efficient by building an outline before you start. Write the contents of each Roman numeral at the top of a separate sheet of paper. The Roman numerals will mark off the basic information your teacher requires. Probably in this manner:

I. the question the experiment was designed to answer
II. the procedures you used to find the answers
III. the results
IV. the conclusions that can be drawn from the results

Now proceed to fill in each sheet with the proper information. Stick to the point. Use good, clear sentences, diagrams and chemical formulas where necessary. Do not neglect to use the bold print terms that were in the lab procedure in your report as well.

Lecture

Much of your class time will probably be spent listening to the teacher's lecture, which, as previously mentioned, involves a maximum of listening and far less student participation than in most other classes. In fact, participation may be limited to students asking questions. Still, just like coping with other methods of presentation, special techniques can help make it easier for you to learn and remember material presented in the lecture format of teaching. Good listening and notetaking skills are essential if you are to get the most out of a lecture.

The reason your teacher introduces new material in lecture form is to give you the background you will need for the homework, lab, and further lectures. So you need to do two things: 1) listen to and understand the material being presented and 2) take notes so that you will be able to refer back to this information in the process of doing your homework, labs, and reviews. Knowing that careful attention and concentration at this point will make your life a lot easier in the future, should help to get and keep your attention. In addition, ask the teacher to clear up anything you do not understand perfectly. As usual, such class participation will not only help to keep you awake, but will also make it easier for you to understand, remember, and do well on tests.

Efficient students also take lecture notes. This forces you to pay attention (after all, you cannot write notes to your friends and take good lecture notes at the same time), and gives you a record of the lecture that you will need for future work. As usual, take class notes on the right side of the page only.

If this is an introduction of new material, you will have to write more than a further explanation would require, but your teacher will not expect you to come to class already knowing about the topic. The object is to create a record that you, yourself, can decipher later. You do not need to worry about complete sentences or beautiful style. Abbreviations are fine, if you know what they are. Be sure to note how this new topic fits into what you already know, and what is new about it. Add everything your teacher writes on the board, and anything that is stressed. The main points of the lecture are important.

If the lecture explains more about textbook material previously covered as homework, you still need to listen well and take good notes. In this case, the teacher has a right to assume that you come to the lecture with the background presented in the textbook. This means that you will have a very hard time staying involved in the lecture if you have not done the homework. If everything seems too new, or there are too many missing links, you will get lost, bored, and may well "turn off."

❑ If you have a few extra minutes before class begins, help yourself "tune back in" to last night's homework, get your mind on science and off the last class by going over your bold print term cards. Now that you are involved, you need to stay that way and help yourself understand and remember to the fullest by asking questions and taking notes.◆

Ask questions about anything you did not understand in the homework as well as anything that is not clear in the lecture. One word of caution: ❑ Ask questions about the topic the teacher is talking about right now, not what he or she was discussing half an hour ago. Otherwise, your question interrupts the flow of the lecture and the teacher will be annoyed rather than pleased with your participation.◆ If the teacher does not get near the topic of your question, wait until the class is over to ask your question.

Even if you have fully understood the lesson give yourself extra feedback by volunteering answers to questions other students ask. ❑ And do not "tune out" when the teacher calls on someone else. Use the opportunity to be involved 100% of the time by saying the answer to yourself when another student gives the "official" answer.◆

Your other major task is to take notes during the lecture. This is not even an extra chore. You will need the class notes for your reviews, even if you understood all of the homework assignment. The method discussed below involves a minimum of writing, so that you will not lose the thread of the lecture while you take notes. Remember, you used left side of looseleaf paper for your textbook notes. The right side will now be used for class notes.

Label the right page opposite the first page of the day's textbook notes with the chapter title under discussion and the date of the class session. Write down **only the new information the teacher adds to what you already know from the textbook**. Be sure to include any new terms the teacher writes on the blackboard in your notes.

You will not have time during a lecture to organize your class notes into beautiful paragraphs or even sentences, but there is no need to do that — phrases with lots of abbreviations will do very nicely. (Just make sure you can decipher your own abbreviations afterwards.)

The next time you have a lecture, practice taking class notes with this system. Be sure to answer the questions on the homework the night before, and go over your bold print term cards before class, so that you have all the raw materials at hand to be a good listener and take good class notes.

Review

Putting in a lot of study time, but not remembering much, does not improve you test grades. As we discussed in Chapter I, the way to get the most out of each minute of your study time is to review frequently, regularly, and with a system that concentrates on learning what you do not know yet, rather than relearning what you already know.

To be really effective, **you need to review when there is no immediate pressure on you.** You can probably think of many other things that seem more important or more fun. There is a great temptation to wait until a test is pending before reviewing. If you give in, though, you put yourself in the unfortunate situation of having to "cram" all that material into a short period of time before the test. You can spare yourself a lot of effort and anxiety if you build regular, frequent reviews into your normal study routine. If you do that, the results will soon be so obvious, that getting yourself to do it will be easy.

Review During Homework

Earlier in this chapter we covered the "little" reviews that should be part of doing your homework. There were two steps at this level of the pyramid to good grades: pausing just a minute after studying each numbered section of your textbook and reviewing at the end of your homework session.

Review Before Class

The review before a lab period has to be different than before a lecture. Both are covered earlier in this chapter, and serve to prepare you to get the most out of the class period. Review before lab by looking over the most obvious stumbling blocks: warnings, measurements, and illustrations. If you are about to have a lecture, read over the bold print term cards.

Review Before Tests

Now we get to the new material. Reviewing before tests sounds like the most difficult review, but you are in for a pleasant surprise **if** you have done a good job up to this point. You are about to reap a well-deserved reward. You will not have to spend as much time studying for the test, and the test results will be much better than it would have been if you had not been such an efficient student.

❑ To begin with, as soon as a test is announced, enter on your assignment sheet the date, the material to be covered, and any other information about the test the teacher gives you.◆ Then write "study for science test" under the two school days before the test. You will not need to spend the entire two days studying for the test, but it is best to allow yourself two days so that you can start your own private reviewing the night before any in-class review. This lets you make maximum use of the in-class review.

Review the Night Before the In-class Review

❑ Start by checking your assignment sheet to make sure you are studying the correct material.◆ Get as far as you can (in no more than an hour and a half) in this review program on the night before the in-class review. The idea is to find out if there is any material that you do not yet understand, and should therefore ask you teacher to clarify during the in-class review; and to learn enough so that you can use the in-class review as an ungraded test. On the night before the test, you should study items you missed during the in-class review and continue the review program where you left off the night before.

Now, on to the review program. If your teacher gave you a study sheet, you are in luck: the teacher has already sorted out the information that he or she considers most important, and is therefore the raw material for test questions. This relieves you of responsibility for items **not** covered on the study sheet. If your teacher did not provide a study sheet, you have to use the chapter review questions in your textbook for this purpose. The chapter review questions are unfortunately not as correlated to what your teacher considers most important (and will include on the test) as your teacher's own study sheet would be, but they are better than having no questions with which to structure your review.

There are generally terms and essay questions on both teacher-provided study sheets and chapter reviews. There may be fill-in-the-blank and multiple choice questions (particularly on chapter reviews) as well. Treat each of these types of questions in a different way in making your study materials and in studying from them.

First, make 3x5 vocabulary cards for each of the terms on your study sheet or chapter review using the same system (described on p. 62) that you used to make vocabulary cards while you were studying your homework assignment. If you did a good job on your homework, you have **already** made 3x5 cards for most or all of the terms you need to study for the test. What a nice reward for the work you put in at homework time!

Next, make yourself a work sheet for the essay questions using the system (described on p. 63-64) you used to incorporate the self-check questions into a work sheet for taking notes, only this time you can use both sides of the paper. You do not need to bother with the fill-in-the-blank and/or multiple-choice questions at this time.

Now you are ready to study. Start with the terms, because they will help "get you into" studying for the test. Use the **quizzing** and **memorizing procedures** discussed on pp. 64 and 65 to remember the most in the shortest time, but spend no more than fifteen minutes on the cards the first day. You may be surprised at how many terms you already know.

The next item is to answer the essay questions. The point is to get accurate answers to the questions and at the same time to find out what you already know (so that you can put your energy into relearning what you do not yet know). Beautiful sentences and paragraphs are not needed at this point, but do use your own words, since they are easier to remember. Get as far as you can from memory. Check your answers; then in red correct answers you missed and fill in any information you did not know using your homework and class notes as well as lab reports or summaries. This system tells you right away the next time you work with the essay questions what information you did not know the first time around and therefore need to relearn (everything in red). If you have done a good job up to this point on homework and in class, the information will be right there and **you do not need to reread the textbook**. This saves much time and effort while studying for a test, a time when every minute counts.

Finally, if you have fill-in-the-blank and/or multiple choice questions, answer these right in your book or on your study sheet. Again, get as far as you can from memory. Then look back in your notes and lab reports or summaries to check your answers. On a separate sheet of paper rewrite in red any questions that you missed. Just as with the essay question, you want to use this stage of your review to find out what you do not yet know and to get a 100% correct version of these items. In this way you will be able to study only what you do not yet know at the next stage. Try to get this far on your first night of review.

The next step is to relearn anything you have forgotten. You are, however, not wasting an instant reviewing what you already know. Start by putting the 3x5 cards in the "**don't know**" pile through the familiar **quizzing** and **memorizing** procedures until you know three quarters of the original list of terms from your teacher-provided study sheet or the chapter review. Put the remaining vocabulary cards into a pile labeled "**problems**" to review whenever you have a spare minute between now and test time.

Then turn to the essay questions. Start by slowly reading aloud five times the questions and answers to each question that has any red writing on it (indicating that you did not know some or all of the information required). Try to etch the answers into your memory as you read them. Now you are ready to test whether you have relearned any of the information you missed the first time around. Cover up the answer to each question with a sheet of paper. Write the complete answer out on the cover sheet from memory. Compare your new answer to the correct version under the cover sheet. If your answer is 100% correct, put a big C in front of the essay question on the work sheet. If you left out some information or parts of your answer were wrong, restudy your correct answer by again reading it aloud slowly and trying to etch the correct answer into your mind. These questions now go into the "**problems**" pile right on top of the 3x5 cards.

Finally, study the fill-in-the-blank and multiple choice questions that you rewrote in red (because you did not know the answers the last time around) by reading both questions and answers aloud five times. Then retake the questions. Correct your answers. Rewrite any items missed, restudy missed items by slowly reading both question and answer aloud; and put the rewritten questions on the **"problem"** pile. Fasten the pile with a large paper clip, and go over these **"problems"** whenever you have an extra minute between now and test time.

In-Class Review

Having done your own review, you are in a good position to get the most out of an in-class review: you can use it as a sort of ungraded test to find out if you know everything you need to know. Write information you missed during the in-class review on a sheet of paper labeled **"did not know during in-class review."** Both of these aspects of in-class review are important, because anything covered on the in-class review is likely to be on the test.

People who answer and ask questions get the most out of in-class reviews. Make sure to use the opportunity to get all your questions answered. ❑ In addition, volunteer answers, and use the trick of answering mentally when classmates are called on to participate 100%.◆

Review the Night Before the Test

While the students who have not worked as efficiently as you are trying feverishly to study for the test the night before, you have a relatively easy task ahead of you: All you need to do is study the items on the **"did not know during in-class review"** work sheet you made for yourself during the in-class review, and continue your review where you left off last night.

Put a good deal of effort into relearning items missed on the in-class review. They will very likely be on the test. Turn each item you did not know during in-class review into a question and write it on a new sheet of paper. Then use all the materials in your notes, lab reports, and 3x5 cards to answer each question. Write out the answers and study them by reading them over carefully five times. Test yourself by writing the answers on a sheet of scratch paper from memory. Compare, and relearn until you know everything. Of course, if the item is a figure, learn to label or draw it from memory (whichever your teacher requires).

Now continue your own review following the directions above. If you have any time left, go over the items in the **"problems"** pile by reading both questions and answers aloud.

You are done. Get a sound night's sleep and eat a good breakfast in the morning. You are all set to go into the test confident, thoroughly prepared, with a smile on your face, and looking forward to the opportunity to prove what you have learned.

Taking Science Tests

The grade in science courses is generally determined by the individual grades you get on tests, quizzes and lab reports, with tests making up the biggest part of the final grade. This part of Chapter III will show you how to adapt the general principles of good test-taking discussed in Chapter I to your science course.

Through the various reviews, you have thoroughly learned the material that will be on the test. ❑ You have also had a good night's sleep and a good breakfast.◆ Your task now is to set up the best possible conditions for taking the test, so that you have that calm, cool, confident frame of mind that is necessary to get good test grades. ❑ Give yourself all the breaks you can. Get to class in plenty of time with all the materials you will need and no others.◆

Objective Questions

This type of question typically involves a large number of items dealing with a wide range of isolated bits of information. Speed is important for doing well on objective questions. You can get this speed by thoroughly knowing the material you will be tested on — the answers should be on the tip of your tongue — and by being an efficient test-taker. Objective questions require slow, accurate reading, but not much writing.

Do **not** try to gain speed by hasty reading of the questions or directions. If you misread either, you will get little credit for your answers.

❑ After reading the directions, go through each objective section of the test answering all the questions you know right off the bat. Do not stop to think about questions you do not know. Just put a pencil check mark in the margin, so you can find unanswered questions quickly, and go on. When you have answered all the items you can and you have some time remaining, go back and answer as many of the checked items as you can. Erase the check mark as you complete the question. But again, do not spend a long time thinking about any one item; it wastes time you will need for the other sections.◆

❑ In doing the objective questions, be on the lookout for "gifts." It is very hard for teachers to write a large number of objective questions without giving away answers to some other questions. Students can take advantage of such unintentional helps. It is perfectly fair. When you find an answer to a question that you checked earlier in the test, quickly turn back and answer the earlier question before you forget.◆

In the last five minutes before handing in the test, go back and answer as many of the remaining checked items as you can. Unless there is a penalty for guessing, there is no advantage in leaving any blanks at this point. One word of caution. ❑ **Never change an objective answer unless you are 100% sure the new answer is correct.** Your first hunch is more likely to be right than a second guess. Do not be one of the many people who change correct answers into wrong ones!◆

Drawing and Labeling

Part of the test may be to make drawings or label diagrams or figures that come out of the textbook or lab work. The best advice here is to do a slow, careful job on the test. Again, careful reading is absolutely essential. Before drawing or labeling anything, read the question all the way through to find out what it is all about. Then draw and/or label the required graphic. Check off each item you are to include or label as soon as you do it. This keeps your place, and avoids accidentally leaving out anything.

Essay Questions

Essay questions in science courses require the clear, concise writing that scientists use. The practice you got in writing lab reports and answering essay questions at the end of each chapter should provide you with useful models.

Because you did a good job reviewing, you will know what to write about. ❑ Making a mini-outline of the major points you want to cover helps you to stay on the subject and include all of the information required.◆ Have a topic sentence in each paragraph; the rest of the sentences in that paragraph should expand on the idea presented in the topic sentence in a few well-chosen words. Good, clear sentences are a plus. Save time by sticking to the point. Do not just write anything that comes into your head in the hope the teacher will eventually find **something** that is useful in your answer.

If at first you know only a little about the essay question, write everything you do know and leave space to add more if you remember additional, **relevant** information later. If — and this is unlikely if you have reviewed well — you cannot remember anything, write the question number in the margin, leave a half page blank, and go on. **Do not** spend a lot of time thinking about these problem questions. Otherwise you will be short of time answering later questions about which you do know something. Use any time you have left for this section to go back and answer, or answer more completely, any question you did not finish.

Conclusion

In this chapter you learned how to be a good science student. We saw that this requires adapting your own reading and writing techniques to the "scientific style" with its long, often Latin-based words and concise, clear, non-repetitive writing.

In doing your homework, it is important to use the scientist's slow, careful, "back-and-forth" method in reading the textbook, and to answer the questions. You also learned ways to stay involved and take notes during class sessions, which often take the form of lectures.

In preparing for labs it is essential to go over the procedures the night before. In addition, it is important to review possible trouble spots before the lab begins. A systematic method of working helps to achieve that calm, purposeful frame of mind conducive to avoiding mistakes, making accurate observation, finishing the lab on time, and writing a good lab report.

As far as reviews are concerned, in science courses you should add one extra review to the usual sequence: after reading each numbered section in the textbook do a minute's mental review of the important points. This can almost double what you remember.

Finally, you learned efficient ways to take tests in science courses. Careful reading and clear, precise writing will lead not only to an improvement in your science grades, but will also have you thinking and observing like a scientist in no time.

REFERENCES

Baldridge, Kenneth P. *Baldridge Reading Instruction Materials.* Greenwich, CT: 1977.

Pauk, Walter. *How to Study in College.* 2nd ed. Boston: Houghton Mifflin, 1974.

Pauk, Walter. *Successful Scholarship.* Englewood Cliffs, NJ.: Prentice-Hall, 1966.

Robinson, H. Alan. *Teaching Reading, Writing, and Study Strategies: the Content Areas.* 3rd ed. Boston: Allyn and Bacon, 1983.

Thomas, Ellen Lamar and Robinson, H. Alan. *Improving Reading in Every Class.* 3rd. ed. Boston: Allyn & Bacon, 1982.

CHAPTER IV

HISTORY

LITTLE THINGS THAT HELP

1. Do all the "Little Things" mentioned in Chapter I.
2. Before doing the actual assignment: read the conclusion of the previous chapter, the title, introduction, conclusion, and review questions of the current chapter.
3. While reading the textbook, make a list of two or three questions you can ask in class the next day.
4. Make a "Bold Print Terms" list.
5. Keep up with the news.
6. Write notes on the textbook on the **left side** of the paper only. Take class notes on the **right side**. This way you only need to write down information in class that is **not** in the textbook notes, making it easier to keep up with the information presented by the teacher.

Introduction

This chapter will show you how to develop the skills needed to become a good history student. Being a good history student is not an accident. Nor is it a matter of suddenly becoming much smarter. In fact, it is not terribly difficult to do a few things that will make a big difference in your performance. If you follow the directions in this book, put in daily effort, are organized, and use your time well, you will see improvement in your history grades.

As is true of any field, the key to success in history is learning the most in the shortest time, and with the least effort. Being an efficient worker in any subject requires having the proper tools and equipment available, and knowing what to do at every stage of the process. Part of the basic message of this chapter is that being a good history student is not really different from being a good athlete, carpenter, or math student.

There is one big difference between a good student and a successful worker in other fields, however: You have to make the tools yourself. Textbook notes, class notes, etc. are part of your tool kit and the better you get at making them, the more efficient you will become as a history student.

The system for getting good history grades presented in this book is like the pyramid shown on the next page. The easiest way to get to the top (good history grades) is to do a super job at each level in turn. At each level you will make the tools that will help you to be efficient on the next level. The levels are the bold-print subdivisions of this chapter. (There is also an introduction, a section discussing tasks and difficulties involved in studying history and conclusion, which are not part of the pyramid.) Each describes what you need to do to become an efficient history student, tells you the advantages of doing things in this way, and, finally, gives you guided practice.

You will find that the new skills build on and utilize the ones you have already mastered. In fact, as you understand how to be an efficient student your skills will increase like a snowball: each successive one is easier to learn and the payoff greater than with the one before. And the habits that help you become a good history student will help you with other subjects and thus give you an extra bonus for your efforts.

Still, learning complicated skills is not easy. Like learning to play the higher levels of a video game, many of the skills described here will take some time and effort to master. However, this is not true of the "Little Things" suggestions at the beginning of the chapter. To keep yourself from getting frustrated and discouraged, start off with the easy things listed in the "Little Things" section. Improving the "Little Things" will provide you with the motivation needed to put effort and time into learning the more difficult skills.

After making the "Little Things" part of you studying efforts, concentrate on learning to read your textbook and taking good notes (pp. 85ff). When you have done the homework well, you have laid the groundwork for being an attentive, active class participant. So the next step will be to learn how to get the most out of class work (pp.100-04) and so on through the chapter.

Pyramid to Good Grades in History

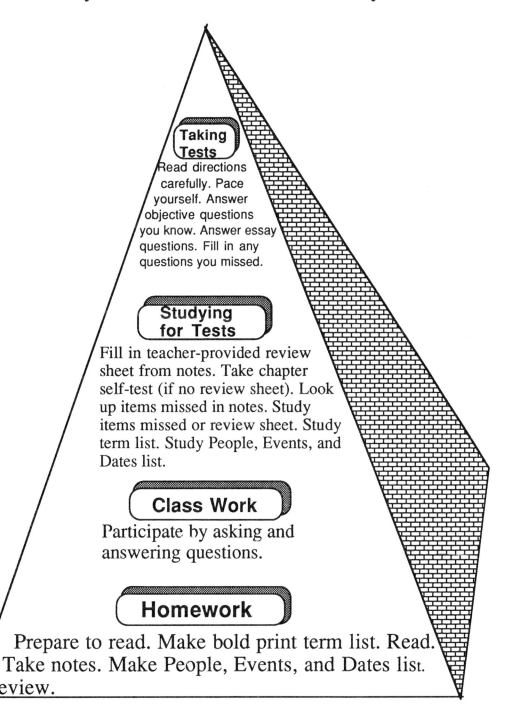

Taking Tests

Read directions carefully. Pace yourself. Answer objective questions you know. Answer essay questions. Fill in any questions you missed.

Studying for Tests

Fill in teacher-provided review sheet from notes. Take chapter self-test (if no review sheet). Look up items missed in notes. Study items missed or review sheet. Study term list. Study People, Events, and Dates list.

Class Work

Participate by asking and answering questions.

Homework

Prepare to read. Make bold print term list. Read. Take notes. Make People, Events, and Dates list. Review.

Tasks and Difficulties Involved in Studying History

To study history effectively you will need to overcome some difficulties and develop some special skills. One problem is the feeling that the subject has little to do with your own life. Another is that the textbook will contain a lot of long, sophisticated words and present information in less specific and concrete ways than a typical math or science book. Many students have difficulty deciding what is an important fact, what is information used to back up these facts, and what is transitional, human-interest, or "filler" material in a history textbook.

As a general rule, the more you know about a subject, the easier it is to read and to remember what you have read. If you regularly read a newspaper or news magazine, watch the news on television, or read historical novels you will soon recognize many of the words and ideas that your teacher and the textbook use. (Just watch how often terms like "gross national product," "recession," or "super power rivalry" appear in the news.) A lot of the ideas and issues that are important today were also important in the period that you are studying. This includes, for example, issues like "nationalism," "revolution," "inflation," or "balancing the budget."

So, if you know nothing at all about the subject of the chapter, read a short entry in an encyclopedia. Ten minutes spent on this kind of extra effort can make reading the textbook much easier and more effective, saving you time in the long run. For example, if the chapter is on the "Age of Exploration," look up the names of some of the explorers that are discussed in the chapter. This information helps you to read the words more easily and to understand the concepts presented.

Doing these things will help you to understand the textbook when you study it. You might also put your imagination to work while you read. Picture the people and events discussed in your mind as if it were a movie. What was life like for a person your age? What might you be doing on a typical day at the hour you are studying? What would you do for fun? What would you eat for dinner? What are you worried about? How would your family have functioned a hundred or two hundred years ago? What kind of living space would you have? At what age would you have to go to work? Doing what? Would you be going to school? What would you be studying? Using your imagination to make history "come alive" helps you relate to the material and makes it much more interesting.

Homework

You will have noticed that point 2 of the "Little Things That Help" handles the problem of reading the textbook in your history course. Understanding the textbook, and doing the homework that is based on the textbook reading, are the first steps to good grades in history courses.

The purpose of assigning textbook reading as homework is so that you will already know a lot about the subject when it is discussed or reviewed in class the next day. In history courses, a successfully completed homework assignment really means having understood and remembered the textbook reading. Like other school work reading a textbook is easier when you have a system or plan of action. The most efficient way of reading a history textbook is to divide the task into three parts: 1) preparation, 2) reading and taking notes, and 3) review.

Unfortunately, many students decide that homework is the one area where the pressure is off and one can get by with little effort. After all, few teachers give quizzes specifically on homework, and the next test seems a long way off. However, **doing your homework carefully and thoroughly is the way to get the most mileage out of the effort you put into your school work**. Well-prepared homework is the bottom level on the pyramid that leads to good history grades, because it helps you to know what is going on in class the next day, and gives you good material to work with when studying for the test. That, in turn, will help you to pay attention, participate in class, take good class notes (again, a tool to study for the test), remember what you have learned, and finally, achieve your goal of getting good grades.

History textbooks contain not only information, but also many aids and helpful hints that you can take advantage of; each chapter probably includes an introduction, a conclusion, headings, review questions, and graphics. In addition, a glossary and index are probably found at the end of the book. Unfortunately, students who have trouble with textbooks tend to ignore these features because they assume that the textbook can only be read like a novel straight down the page from beginning to end. This is a fundamental mistake, because it ignores the aids put in by the author to help the student.

The purpose of a history textbook is to help students understand what has happened and why it is important. The level of difficulty of a history textbook can be deceptive. History textbooks are written in narrative form, so that the text seems to "flow along" like a novel. The authors write in this style because history is, in many ways, a "story," and because they need to explain how they arrived at their conclusions.

This means that history textbooks contain a lot of information, but not all of it is equally important. The author will attempt to guide the reader through this thicket of information by being especially well organized. In fact, history textbooks are almost always written from a strict outline, and headings and other indicators help you see the outline the author used. All of the paragraphs under a heading will relate to the subject announced in the heading. Each paragraph has a main idea or topic sentence, with the rest of the paragraph being supporting material. This arrangement of sentences helps you decide not only what is most important, but also how the main item is backed up; in other words what information the author uses to show that the topic sentence is true.

Preparation for Reading

Since studying your history book is not the same as reading a novel, it is useful to do a number of things before you actually start to read the chapter even if you are somewhat familiar with the topic. For example, your reading will be much more successful if you know how the material in the current chapter fits in with what came before. ❑So before starting to read your assignment spend a few minutes **reading the conclusion of the previous chapter**; as well as the **title, introduction, section headings, conclusion and review questions of the current chapter**.

Start with the conclusion of the previous chapter. This will remind you what the last chapter was about and help you to see how the new information presented in the current chapter is related to and built on what you read earlier. Look over your class notes from today as well. Your teacher may have given you a valuable introduction, and you do not want to disregard any help that comes your way.

Now turn to the chapter that you were assigned and read the title, the introduction and the section headings. Read the introduction with the idea, "in this section the author is trying to fit the new material into what I already know, and is trying to give me a preview of the coming chapter, so that I will know what is significant when I get to it." The headings are actually the major points (the Roman numerals) from the author's own outline. In the textbook they are printed in larger letters, written in a different color, or highlighted in some other way to catch your eye and make you notice them. The paragraphs that follow should all deal with the subject indicated in the heading.

Next, turn to the conclusion. This is actually a recap of the chapter. Here the author reviews the main points of the chapter and relates them to each other. Read the conclusion with the idea that the author is telling you what he or she considers to be the highlights of the chapter and what they are supposed to mean. Knowing the major points covered gives you "hooks" on which to hang more detailed information you will read later.

Most textbooks include a set of review questions at the end of sections and/or chapters. Looking at the review questions before reading the assignment will help you to become familiar with the material to be covered in the chapter. You will already know which points the author thinks are important, and can spot them when you turn to the actual reading.◆

Apply the prereading process to tonight's history homework. This first time may take a little longer, but once you get used to it, you will move along much more quickly, and you will find that this way of studying helps you get the most out of your time and effort. The steps are summarized below for easy reference.

Step 1 - Read the conclusion of the previous chapter.

Step 2 - Read the title, introduction, and section headings of the current chapter.

Step 3 - Read the conclusion of current chapter.

Step 4 - Read the review questions of the current chapter.

Making a Bold Print Term List

Now you are ready for the next step. It will not take you long to discover that history textbooks and courses present you with large numbers of new and sometimes foreign words. To help students with this problem, most textbooks use bold print (fat, very black print) or italics (thin print that is written at an angle) to highlight new and important terms. To understand what the author has written, you have to understand these words.

Making a list and writing down the author's definitions isolates the words in bold print, and helps you to learn the terms. Doing this **before** you actually start reading will make it much easier for you to read, understand, and remember the material presented in the chapter.

A good way of making a Bold Print Terms List is to fold a sheet of notebook paper in half lengthwise, and make it look like the example below. Go through your assignment and write the bold print words on your list. Leave one line blank in between each term and its definition, to clearly separate the items like the sample below.

SAMPLE BOLD PRINT TERM LIST

Chapter , pp.

Terms   *Definitions*

1. business cycle   recurring states of
                                     prosperity and hard times

2. prosperity   good times — people have
                                     jobs, money to spend,
                                     business is good

Reading the Textbook

Reading history textbooks means coping with a number of problems. The first is the use of sophisticated words and terms. History textbooks often use these in different and sometimes confusing ways. In science and mathematics textbooks new terms tend to have quite specific meanings. On the other hand, in the stories or novels you read for English class, the authors try to stimulate your own imagination in interpreting the action and the characters, rather than providing scientifically correct descriptions. The way history textbooks are written lies somewhere in between these two examples.

Sometimes history terms are quite specific. For example, "the American Revolution" describes the series of events whereby the United States achieved independence from Great Britain. But the meaning of the term "industrial revolution" is much more complex and less precise. This is even more true of phrases like, "the atmosphere of the times," a term you will often encounter in history textbooks. Here the authors are attempting to characterize a certain feeling, not a specific series of events.

Essentially what you are encountering here is the vocabulary used by writers of history textbooks. The easiest way to approach getting meaning out of a history book is to compare reading with trying to solve a mystery or deciphering a secret code. Words like parliamentarism, constitutionalism, monetarism, or agricultural price parity, for example, may be a problem. As with any subject, part of becoming a good student in history is to learn these code words.

Actually, long words are nothing to be afraid of. To begin with, they are usually pronounced exactly the way they look, so you may recognize the meaning of the words by merely pronouncing them. Step 1 in reading long, sophisticated words, then, is to **look at them carefully**. Resist the impulse to just skip over them. Looking at such words carefully and pronouncing them may be all you need to go on and read the rest of the sentence.

If you do not recognize the meaning of a word after looking at it carefully and trying to pronounce it, the next step is to **take the word apart**. Do you recognize any little words within the word? Take off the prefix or suffix and see if the word now becomes familiar. If the word still does not seem familiar to you, break it up into syllables and pronounce each syllable in turn. If that still does not help, write them on an extra sheet of paper. Isolating the parts of a word often makes the word clear. If you now think you do know the word, read the rest of the sentence. If the sentence makes sense you have probably understood the word with which you originally had trouble.

To repeat, there are only two steps to pronouncing an unknown word:
   1) Look at the word carefully.
   2) Take the word apart.

Of course, even if you can pronounce the word, you may still not know what it means. You have gotten to second base, but that does not yet score a run. If you can pronounce the word, but do not know its meaning, take the following steps in order. (They are listed from the easiest and quickest to the most difficult.) **Stop the process when you know what the word means**. Keep going back to step 1 to check if "your" meaning of the word makes sense. If it does, you are probably right.

1) **Read the rest of the sentence**. Often the way a word is used in the sentence makes its meaning clear.

2) Look to **see if this is one of the words on your list of bold print or italicized words**. If so, the meaning should be right next to the

term on your list. In addition, many history textbooks will have an alphabetized glossary at the end of the book that you can check.

3) **Look the word up in the dictionary**. Then add the word to your list of Bold Print terms. Even though the word is not technically in bold print, you did not know it, so you need to put it on a list that you can review regularly so that it will become part of your vocabulary.

Now practice what you have learned as you do your own history assignment. You will find that with a little practice, this system of reading and understanding history material will become second nature to you, and you will not have to check back to know what the various steps are. Until then, consciously go through the steps every time you have trouble with a word.

Taking Notes on the Textbook

Textbook reading in history courses is a time-consuming task if you do it well, and there is not much purpose in doing it at all, if you do not do it well. If you read the material once for your homework assignment, reread it for a quiz and read it a third time for the test, you would not only get sick and tired of the material, but have little time for doing anything else in your life. This is why you need to learn to take notes. Note taking is a process whereby you are condensing the main points of the textbook information into a much shorter form, using your own words.

Taking notes on the textbook reading gets you around the rereading problem and has a number of other advantages as well. You cannot "take notes" on the material if you have not understood what the author wrote (just copying the assigned reading almost word for word is **not** taking notes). So notetaking is a way to test your understanding. The second advantage is that rewriting and condensing the material will help you to remember what you read. Writing something down is always an effective memory aid.

In addition, taking notes will give you a record of the material in the chapter when it comes to reviewing for the test. If you have done a good job taking notes, you will not have to reread the chapter when you are preparing for quizzes and tests. That will **save you a good deal of time** and pay you back for the effort you put in taking notes as part of your homework. Finally, you will already have notes on much of the material the teacher will bring up in class. This helps you know what is going on, and makes it easy to take class notes, because all you will have to write down during class is **new** material.

You will have noticed that we are defining "taking notes" as some form of rewriting the material in the chapter; neither highlighting nor underlining is a good substitute for written notes. The problem with these popular methods of "taking notes" is that they are too easy to do. (Highlighting and underlining can at times be useful, but only for people who are already very good at taking notes and who will not fool themselves into thinking they have taken real notes without actually doing it.) If you are a typical student, highlighting and underlining take little effort on your part, so you tend to mark virtually every word in the text, ending up with a sea of yellow highlighting or underlining. Unfortunately, while recoloring the page you will not have thought about the content or decided what is important and what is not. **It is the mental reworking of the content that makes notetaking such an effective tool for really understanding and remembering the material.**

Now, believe it or not, you are ready to take notes. If your teacher did not tell you what kind of notes to take on your reading you can decide for yourself which method of notetaking will work best for you. No one method has been shown to be better than any other method. Just make sure that you have notes on all parts of the chapter. Whatever note-taking method you use, the idea is to have a short, compressed version of your assignment. To accomplish this, you must think about what you have read, and decide what information is really important, what is supporting evidence, and what is primarily illustrative material. In taking notes you are really writing down your own personal version of the assigned reading. Two methods of taking notes on history textbooks will be presented in this book: outlining and answering the review questions.

Whatever method you use, start by writing the chapter number and title on the top few lines of your paper. Always use only the left side of your paper for notes on the textbook; the right side should be kept free for class notes. If you write left handed, just do the opposite: right side for homework notes and left side for class notes. In either case the idea is that the ring or spiral binder should not interfere with your writing in class.

The advantage of this system is that you have much less writing to do in class: you only have to write down items that are **not** in your homework notes, making it much easier to keep up with the information presented by the teacher. If you look through your homework notes just before class begins, you will have a good idea what is in these notes, and be able to recognize what you already have when it comes up. If you are answering questions prepared by your teacher or the review questions found in your textbook, skip the outlining directions and go right to the next section.

Outlining is probably one of the easiest method to use with history textbooks, because such textbooks are themselves written from an outline. In outlining the text, you are essentially reconstructing the author's own outline. For this reason, the headings in the chapters will become the Roman numerals of your outline. Similarly, the main idea or topic sentence of each paragraph below the heading will become a capital letter. The arguments supporting the main idea form the Arabic numerals, and the details of these arguments the small letters. Indent about an inch for each category, in order to separate clearly the items of similar significance. The further to the right an item is written, the less important it is.

In writing your outline, do not use sentences; they are too long. Phrases and single words and abreviations compress the meaning more and are, therefore, more effective. Just make sure you use only abreviations that you will recognize later.

Practice outlining your current assignment. To give you a picture, a sample from an imaginary chapter has been done for you.

Chapter 5: The Great Depression of the 1930s

I. introduction
   A. depressions in U.S. every 25-30 years
   B. government interference to shorten depressions regarded as bad

II. normal business cycle
   A. made up of recurring stages each paving way for next
   B. length of stages not predictable
   C. prosperity (good times)
      1. easy credit
      2. high profits
      3. factories work near capacity
      4. little unemployment

You should always supplement your outline with a **People, Events, and Dates List.** This list is similar to the Bold Print Terms List you completed earlier. List the people, events and dates you need to know something about on the left-hand side of the paper and try to write three to five facts about each on the right-hand side of your paper opposite the listing. Leave three lines blank in between entries for additional information you may receive in class. Since class material is likely to appear on tests, write this new information in a different color.

There are two good reasons for writing down this many facts. First, you do not know yet what your teacher will consider important — and therefore put on the test — so you need to know as much as possible about each item. Secondly, unless your memory is perfect, having extra information gives you a safety net. Even if you forget some facts, you will still remember enough of them to do well on the test. If you list the items in the order in which they appear in your textbook (including important dates), your "People, Events, and Dates List" also gives you a beautiful chronology — the order in which things happened — something that is particularly useful for history courses.

The beginning of a "People, Events, and Dates List" for an imaginary chapter is shown below. Make a list of your own from the assignment you are working on.

People, Events, and Dates List

Chapter 5

People, Events, and Dates	_Facts_
Herbert Hoover	US President (1928-32) during worst years of depression. Opposed government action to ease depression
1929-1933	years of steep decline
Dec. 1941	US enters World War II. Ends Depression.

You now know and have practiced all the steps you should go through in reading and **outlining** your textbook assignment:

Step 1 - Preparation
> Read the conclusion of the previous chapter.
> Read the title and headings of the current chapter.
> Read the conclusion of the current chapter.
> Read the review questions at the end of the current chapter.

Step 2 - Make a Bold Print Terms List.

Step 3 - Outline the chapter.

Step 4 - Make a People, Events, and Dates List.

Skip past the section on answering review questions and go right to p. 100, the five-minute review that should mark the end of your homework session.

Answering Review Questions

Virtually all history textbooks have review questions either at the end of each section, at the end of the chapters, or both. If you prefer to take notes by answering these questions, here is how to do it. If your teacher prepared questions for you to answer, just substitute those questions for the ones found in the textbook and follow the directions below.

There is a catch, however. In order to answer a question you first have to know what it is asking. History teachers and authors of history textbooks tend to use certain "question" words again and again. Be sure to know exactly what these words mean, because if you do not, your answer will probably be wrong. To help you with this difficulty, listed below are some of these frequently encountered words and their meanings.

discuss = Give an account of the major developments.

compare = How are the circumstances, motivations, personalities, etc. similar for two or more events or developments?

contrast = How are the circumstances, motivations, personalities, etc. different for two or more events or developments?

show the development of = Tell about the changes that have occurred to produce a certain outcome.

cause = What made the event or events happen?

result = What happened because of earlier events or developments?

define = Write what a word or phrase means in this specific context.

describe = Give the essential facts of an event, a development, or an idea.

Learning the words used by history authors and teachers to ask questions **now** has another advantage: When you get to the test, you will know precisely what the teacher is asking!

When you take notes by answering the review questions, it is a good idea to have the questions in front of you as you read the chapter. That way you will not have to constantly interrupt your reading to look back at the questions. Since textbooks usually have two types of questions, make yourself two work sheets. The first work sheet is for **identification questions**, the second for **essay questions**.

For your first work sheet, write down the identification questions for your current assignment. You should try to find at least three facts about each of these items. Leave space to add any extra information your teacher gives you in class.

Many of these items should already be in your "Bold Print Terms" list, making it easy for you to answer the identification questions if you have done a good job on the Bold Print Terms list. **Note:** people who use this system of note-taking do not need to make a "People, Events, and Dates" list, because much of this information will be included as part of the review questions. The beginning of your identification worksheet should look like this: (Be sure to label every page so you can put the pages back in order easily if they accidentally fall out of your ring book.)

Review Questions Chapter 5

SAMPLE IDENTIFICATION QUESTIONS

<u>Social legislation</u>
    1.
    2.
    3.

<u>seller's market</u>

            1.
            2.
            3.

    entrepreneurs
            1.
            2.
            3.

    bank failure
            1.
            2.
            3.

The second work sheet is for **essay questions**. Begin by rewriting the question as a statement. To answer essay questions you will need more space than for identification questions. You will need to write at least a paragraph to fully answer each essay question. Give yourself at least a third of a page for each question. In other words, your work sheet should list no more than three questions per page. Questions with a lot of parts to them will probably require more space, so multi-part questions should only have two to a page. Now go to the review questions in your assignment and reword the questions into statements. An example of what your sheet might look like is shown below. Rewrite your own essay questions as statements in the same way. (You only need to rewrite the question. The original question is in this sample just to show you how to do it.)

Review Questions Chapter 5

SAMPLE ESSAY QUESTIONS

Question: Describe the conditions under which the unemployed had to live during the Great Depression.

Question rewritten as a statement: The conditions under which the unemployed had to live during the Great Depression were:

You now have two work sheets and are ready to read. Read the information under the first heading in your assignment. Read it all the way through before trying to answer any questions. If you read just enough to answer the specific review questions, you will miss some of the author's arguments, and consequently will have a harder time understanding and remembering the chapter contents.

Read the first question on each of your work sheets. (The review questions are often in the same order as the information is presented in the chapter.) Does the first heading give you the information you need? If yes, fill in the answer in your own words.

Although it is harder to do than quoting the author, putting the answers into your own words saves you time and effort in the long run. First of all, you cannot express things you do not understand in your own words, so this activity tests whether you understand the material or need to reread the textbook. The second benefit is that your mental reworking of the information makes it easier to remember later. So think of the effort involved in putting the answer into your own words as an investment. You will get the time back and then some when you study for the test.

If the answers you are looking for are not part of the material under the first heading, read the information under the second heading and so on until you find all the information you need to answer all the review questions.

People who take notes by answering review questions have one advantage over those who take notes by outlining: They have a built-in opportunity to practice answering history questions. Your ability to express yourself in writing is very important in history. Part of your grades on tests are a function of how well you can express what you have learned in writing. Having all the information in your head without being able to put it down on paper will not result in good grades on tests. Therefore, write good, complete sentences that express the information clearly — not one or two word answers. The essay questions should be divided into paragraphs each with a topic sentence.

Your finished work sheets should look something like this sample:

Review Questions Chapter 5

SAMPLE IDENTIFICATION QUESTIONS

Social legislation
   1. includes social security, national welfare system,

unemployment insurance, insurance on bank accounts
2. all meant to help people who lose their jobs, or have savings or investments
3.

seller's market
1. is when goods are easy to sell at a high price
2. makes it easy to have high profits
3.

entrepreneurs
1. are people who make goods or provide services
2.
3.

bank failure
1. occurs when a bank goes out of business
2. if accounts are not insured, the depositors lose their money
3.

Review Questions Chapter 5

SAMPLE ESSAY QUESTION

1. The conditions under which the unemployed had to live during the Great Depression were terrible. During the Great Depression there was no social "safety net" to help those who had lost their jobs: no social security, no national welfare system, no unemployment insurance, no insured bank accounts. If you lost your job, you were not entitled to any help.

People had to accept charity from churches etc. in the form of bread lines, and soup kitchens, or welfare from state and local governments. Many people sold apples or pencils on street corners to make a few cents. In fact bread lines and people selling apples were symbols of the times. Others begged or stole rides on freight trains. The suicide rates went up.

If you are answering either your teachers or the textbook's review questions you should now have done all of the steps that you should go through in reading and taking notes on a textbook assignment:

Step 1 - Preparation
> Read the conclusion of the previous chapter.
> Read the title and headings of the current chapter.
> Read the conclusion of the current chapter.
> Read the review questions at the end of the current chapter.

Step 2 - Make a Bold Print Terms List
Step 3 - Make an identification question work sheet.
Step 4 - Make an essay question work sheet.
Step 5 - Answer the review questions by filling in your work sheets.

With your textbook notes complete you have the information presented in the textbook in two condensed forms. In your "Bold Print Terms list" and your "People, Events, and Dates list," or the identification work sheet, you are taking details out of the context and considering them individually. With your outline or essay questions, on the other hand, you are integrating the details into a whole sequence of events that indicate how the details relate to each other, and what their relative significance is in terms of causes and consequences of longer-term developments. Thinking about, reworking, and writing the material will help you to know what you are talking about the next day in class, remember what you have read, and do well on the test.

Review

Sorry, you're not quite finished with your homework yet. Take five more minutes to reread your bold print terms list and the notes that you have taken (either outline or answering questions). This short review will "fix" the information in your mind, and make remembering it next day during class much easier.

One more suggestion from the "Little Things" list is worth mentioning here. ❑ While you are reading and taking notes on your textbook assignment, it is a good idea to write down questions to ask in class. These can be points that the author has not made quite clear to you, or something that you would like more information about. Preparing such questions will make it easier for you to get started on class participation by letting you prepare something to bring up in class ahead of time.

Having some questions in hand that you know are relevant, because they are actual questions you had while reading the assignment, helps overcome the reluctance many students have to participate in the class discussion. Asking a question does not mean you are stupid. It is not smart to leave such a beautiful opportunity for reviewing the homework for the best students. As we discussed in chapter I, active class participation also makes it easier to pay attention, to remember the subject matter, and to do well on the test.◆

Just one word of caution: Be sure to ask your questions at the time the teacher is dealing with that subject. An easy way to remind yourself where your questions fit in is to make a mark in your textbook notes at such places. **Do not spend the entire period getting your courage up to ask a question on a topic that was discussed half an hour earlier.** If you do this, your efforts will backfire, because your question will disrupt the flow of the class discussion rather than contribute to it, and will be more likely to make the teacher angry rather than impressed.

Classwork

To do a good job during a history class you should do four things:
1 - **Review your textbook notes before class.**
2 - **Be an active listener.**
3 - **Participate positively, and**
4 - **Take good class notes.**

Notice that these four activities are mutually reinforcing: Reviewing your homework notes promotes participation, note-taking and active listening; active listening helps you to take good notes and participate; participation keeps you alert to be an active listener and take good notes; and good class notes will help you when it is time to do your next homework assignment.

Boredom and lack of attention appear when a student knows nothing about the subject being discussed. It is strange but true, that students who did not understand the homework will be bored and inattentive in class the next day, even though they should be paying extra attention in order to understand the material the second time around. This is why the first level on the pyramid of success in history is so important and should take the most time: Homework done well makes you familiar with the subject under discussion in class the next day, helping you to do a good job on this second level (class work).

Active Listening

But what is an "active listener?" Someone who jumps up and down distracting the class, or carries on a private conversation? **No.** An "active listener" is a good receiver of information, and does not interfere with the messages coming in from the teacher. But active listeners are not simple sponges, merely soaking up what is said in class. They think about what is said, and mentally work with the information.

To be an active listener, you should ask yourself questions. Does this information agree with what you already know? Does it make sense? How does it fit in? Mental reworking and evaluation of the material presented in class helps you to stay alert, to take good class notes, to remember the information, and, finally, to do well on the test. The more you review and think about the information, the easier it is to remember. If you are a passive, rather than an active listener, you are only using half of the instruction you receive.

Class Participation

Now on to class participation. ❑ As mentioned in the preceding chapters, spend any time you have before class gets under way to refresh your homework in your memory. Just looking over the Bold Print Term List should do the trick.◆ The two or three questions you wrote down while doing your homework should also help conquer any shyness you have and help you participate in class. As we discussed in chapter I, class participation helps you to recycle your learning, and remember more for the test. It also helps impress the teacher with your desire to learn.

Class Notes

Broadly speaking, history teachers can be divided into two types: those who pretty much limit themselves to explaining the textbook in class, and those who use lecturing and guided class discussion to add new material to that found in the textbook. In either case, it is essential that you learn to be an active listener, a good participant in class, and to take good class notes.

Good class notes are vital tools, since these are your best record of what the teacher considers important and thus what is likely to be on the test. In addition, if you have the "new material" type of teacher, then you need to be an active listener and an excellent class note-taker, because class is your only chance to get this "extra" information. At this point, you get your first big reward for the hard work you did reading and taking notes the night before. You also get direct payoff from reviewing your textbook before class began: You know what is being discussed, and what is already in your notes, so you will not be rewriting information you already have.

If you have done a good job on the notes you took the night before, then you really only have to concern yourself with two things in the way of classroom notes: 1) **items that the teacher mentions that are already in your notes**, which only need to be marked in some way. Underline or check them right on your textbook notes, to tell you what the teacher thought important enough to mention in class, and 2) **information the teacher gives you on each topic that is <u>not</u> in your textbook notes**, which you will write down on the right hand side of your notebook.

For instance, your textbook under the heading "The Reign of Charlemagne" may have discussed the battles of this emperor, without saying anything about the schools he established. Meanwhile, the teacher might mention the schools, but not say anything **new** about Charlemagne's military campaigns. In this case, all you have to put on the right side of the paper is something like this: <u>Charlemagne</u>: "Established schools mostly to teach children of nobles. Teachers were monks." The information about the military campaigns only needs to be checked or underlined in your textbook notes on the left side of your notebook to let you know that the teacher considered it important. You are going to be very happy that you have a way to tell what your teacher considers important when you start studying for the test.

As we said earlier, always take your class notes on the right-hand side of your notebook paper (unless you write left handed) opposite the same topic in your textbook notes (left side) if possible. If the topic was not in your textbook notes at all, write it on an extra sheet of paper (right side). **Label the first page of each day's class notes with the date and chapter under discussion**. This system takes a lot of paper, but will greatly increase your efficiency when you study for the test, because you will know 1) what the teacher considered important, 2) the information (if any) the teacher added to that found in your textbook and 3) any new topics the teacher brought up. All this is important, since it is the teacher who makes up the test.

There is not much sense trying to take your classroom notes in the same neat manner you used for textbook notes at home. Teachers tend to talk fast, and in the course of the classroom discussion instructor and the students may well skip back and forth between topics. So the material will probably not fit comfortably into an outline, or a set of review questions. Just do your best to get the information down. Here as elsewhere, never try to do the impossible.

If you have trouble reading your own handwriting, or do not get a chance to get everything down in a way that will let you understand your class notes a few weeks later, be sure to start your homework tonight by rewriting your class notes and "filling in the blanks." Remember, if you cannot make sense of your class notes when you study for the test, you will be in very bad shape. Now is the time to make sure your notes are clear. The longer you wait to straighten out your notes, the harder the job will be. Your class notes from the next time your history class meets should look something like the sample notes below.

SAMPLE CLASS NOTES

Note: These should be written on the right side of your paper, directly across from the place where the same subject is discussed in your textbook notes, which should be on the left side of the paper. If you have taken good textbook notes, there may be a lot of white space in your class notes. You are only adding **new** information.

Anti-cyclical measures also designed to "even out" normal business cycle — smooth out peaks and valleys — and to keep depressions from being so severe. Great Depression was so bad that theory that government should not interfere was changed. If anti-cyclical measures work, no more depressions, recessions at worst.

Charity 2 problems 1) it could not possibly meet the needs of all unemployed and farmers who lost their land, 2) hard for many people, especially those who had never been unemployed before to accept charity

Economists who wanted to interfere with business cycle
said depressions actually involve 2 interrelated problems: 1) problem of the economy performing so poorly - that can be helped through anti-cyclical measures, 2) problem people have when they lose their livelihood - social legislation helps them

Film strip Many of the unemployed really didn't know where their next meal was coming from or where to spend the night.

In summary, there are four major benefits you get as a student from doing a good job in class. First, active listening means paying attention, and by paying attention you will inevitably learn and remember more. Second, you will find it much easier to study for and get good grades on the test, which is sure to come, because you will have good material from which to study. Third, your teacher, too, will come to think of you as a good student. And finally, since we often do what others expect of us, if the teacher thinks of you as a good student, you are in fact well on your way to being one.

Studying for Tests

The best notes are not much good if you cannot remember the information in them when it comes to quizzes and tests. As we already discussed in Chapter I, if you wait until the test is announced to review, you will have forgotten almost all of the material. That is just not an efficient way to use your valuable study time.

The way out of the memory problem, as usual, is a spaced, planned system of reviewing what you have learned, so that you will remember most of it, instead of forgetting most of it. The best and easiest way to study for a test is to start the process with a five-minute review right after you finish your homework. Next, review for a few minutes before class starts, and recycle your learning during class through active participation.

Then when it comes to studying for the test you can start to reap the rewards for all of the work you have done: You understood the homework, have good homework and class notes, and have already recycled your learning three times. You have everything you need to accomplish the goal for this level of the pyramid — to learn the material so well that even the extra pressure and tension of test day will not get you rattled and make you forget what you have learned. The nice thing is that you will not have to work as hard or spend as much time studying for the test as you would have otherwise, and your chances of success are a whole lot greater!

You have already accomplished three of the five pillars of good test scores: well-done homework, good class notes, and periodic review. If you accomplish the other two (planning your study time, and systematic test review) as well, it would be extremely hard **not** to improve your tests grades. Unfortunately, the reverse is equally true: If you do not study until test time, poor grades are almost automatic. Miracles do happen, but do not count on it. **Good students do not wait for miracles, they make sure that they have done everything they themselves can do to prepare the way for good grades.**

Planning Your Study Time

The purpose of planning your study time is to avoid having work bunch up on you; and so that you get the maximum benefit from the time you invest. If you wait until the last minute to do a particular task, chances are something else important will compete for the needed time. It might be a test or a big project in another class, but it might also be something unrelated to school, like a concert or a big date. The way to get around this problem is to look continuously at the tasks coming up and then work ahead when you have extra time, rather than quitting work early, and just relaxing until the next deadline puts tremendous pressure on you again.

The way to get maximum benefit out of every minute of your study time is to study for the test in two sessions, rather than one. Start the night before the teacher schedules the in-class review. That way you get the most out of the in-class review as well.

Systematic Test Review

The actual review process before tests has three parts: first review at home, in-class review, and second review at home. Start your first at-home review no later than the night before the in-class review. ❑ Check your assignment book to make sure you know precisely what will be covered on the test; do not waste a second studying the wrong thing.◆ Then review the words typically used in history questions. If you have not already learned what these words mean in the context of history, take a few minutes and do it now. If you do not know precisely what the teacher is asking, your chance of answering correctly are slim.

First At-home Review

Gather all the tools you need to prepare for the test: your homework notes (outline or questions) with the class notes on the other side, your bold print term list, and (if you outlined) your "people, events, and dates" list. Then follow the routine described below. Your object is to avoid the frustrated complaint, "I studied for hours, but I failed the test anyway!" If you have followed the directions up to this point, you will be able to spend your entire review time actually studying for the test and not waste your time worrying about it.

Your job at this point is to make a tool that will let you quiz yourself, so that you can determine what you already know and what needs further study. In this way, you will not fall into the trap of spending time going over material you already know.

If your teacher provided a study sheet, your life is easy. The teacher has indicated on that sheet exactly what he/she wants you to learn, and therefore what is fair game to put on the test. If the teacher did not provide you with a study sheet, use the chapter review questions provided by the textbook for this purpose.

Write each identification or short-answer item from the study sheet or chapter review questions on the front of a 3x5 card using big, clear letters and your favorite color. Find the three or more facts you need to remember about each item and write it on the back of the appropriate card.

You want to get all the mileage you possibly can out of all that work you have already done, so check if you already have the information your need in your notes, or on any of your lists. Highlight in yellow any information that you indicated in your notes was discussed in class. This is the minimum your teacher wants you to know. Be sure to include all of it.

If you have done a good job up to this point almost everything you need will be right there. However, **if you did not take good notes, you are in serious trouble**. When you are done, put the cards in a pile labeled test **don't know**. Cards stay in that pile until you prove to yourself in the final at-home review that you know the information. The last thing you need to do with the 3x5 cards at this point is to turn them all so that the front faces up and put them into alphabetical order. This will help you find the card you need in a hurry so you can add any information you do not already have during the in-class review.

Now turn to the essay-type questions. Write each potential essay question listed on the study sheet or chapter review questions at the top of a piece of notebook paper. Put all the information you can gather from your homework and class notes on one side of the paper only. Again make sure to include and highlight all of the information that you indicated in your notes was discussed in class. Leave one line between different pieces of information. This approach saves you time in the next round when you will reorganize this information into essay form. You'll be able to cut and tape, rather than having to rewrite. Should you need more space, just use more sheets of paper. Be sure to staple all sheets belonging to the same question together to avoid any chance of confusion.

If you do not find at least enough information to write three good paragraphs, you have to go back to the section in the textbook where the subject was discussed to get more information. Use the index at the back of the book to find the place in a hurry. **Do not reread the whole chapter.**

Finally, staple a blank sheet of paper to each essay question. Put a big yellow highlighter mark at the top of that page to indicate that all of this information was discussed in the in-class review. The extra sheet gives you a place to write any information that is brought up in class that you do not have yet.

A word of warning: Do **not** assume you can read your teacher's mind and study only part of the possible essay questions. Chances are, the questions on the test will be the ones you did **not** study for.

In-class Review

You are now ready for the in-class review. Take your yellow highlighter, the 3x5 cards, and your essay question sheets to class with you. Pay super attention. Remember, the teacher scheduled the review to help you understand the material and do well on the test. Teachers want their students to do well on tests. After all, good test scores indicate good teaching. In addition, it is likely that your teacher has made up the test before the class review session. As a result, **the teacher will tend to stress items that he or she knows are on the test**, during the review, even if he or she did not set out to do this. Paying attention to these often unconscious and unofficial hints is one of the things that good students do to get their good grades.

When in the course of the review some information is given that belongs on one of the 3x5 cards, put it there and highlight with yellow to indicate the teacher thought it was important enough to bring up in class. Use the extra sheet of paper to give your essay questions the same treatment.

Students without study guides might be faced with items that come up during the review session, but which are not on either the essay sheets or the 3x5 cards. If you know the answer to the question, do not worry about it. If you do not know the answer, write the question and answer on a sheet of paper labeled "What I Didn't Know During In-class Review." There should not be many of these questions.

Super class participation during in-class review pays big dividends. You get a chance to find out what the teacher considers most important (and is therefore likely to have on the test). In addition you can review the material and test yourself without penalty. Make sure to answer frequently and answer mentally when you are not called on.

Second At-home Review

The final part of your systematic test review is your second at-home review. Students who do not have study sheets may very well have come across items that they did not know during the in-class review. They should start their second at-home study session by treating their "What I didn't know during the in-class review" sheet like a teacher-provided study guide. Make 3x5 cards for identification and other short-answer items, and essay sheets for essay-type questions as you did during the first at-home study session. Then proceed with the study plan described below.

Start with the 3x5 cards that are still all together in the **don't know** pile. Look at the front side of each card in turn and write the items that you remember from the back on a piece of scrap paper. Concentrate particularly on etching the items your teacher considered particularly important (the ones highlighted in yellow) into your memory by highlighting them in yellow on your sheet of scrap paper as well. You can heighten the effectiveness of your efforts even further by reciting the information as you write it.

Now find out how good your memory is. Turn the 3x5 card over and see if you remembered **at least** all of the highlighted items and have the same items highlighted on the scrap paper. If so, put the card in a new pile labeled **know**. Do not put the card on the **know** pile until you know **at least all of the highlighted information**. Keep repeating the process with the cards you do not yet know, but keep the sessions short — no more than twenty minutes at a time.

After you have spent twenty minutes working on the 3x5 cards, turn to organizing the essay questions before you do another 3x5 card session. This step is not hard to do, in fact, the task probably takes much longer to explain than it does to actually do. To make the directions easier to follow, we will discuss the process for the question, "Discuss the conditions under which the unemployed had to live during the Great Depression."

Work on one question at a time. Start by cutting the question and each separate piece of information off the sheets of paper on which you wrote them during your first at-home review and the in-class review. This should be easy, because you left a line between entries.

Now you are ready to play solitaire with the pieces of paper you have cut out. For the next operation seat yourself at a table, so you will have room to spread out your materials. Put the slip of paper with the question on it in the middle of the table. Then gather related items together and place them in front of you in columns. Make sure that you have included all highlighted information. This is the minimum you must include in your essay, since it is the information your teacher considered most important. More information is a nice addition, but should not replace the highlighted points.

Now look at each column in turn to discover a theme that ties the related bits of information together. If one of your items turns out to be that theme, all you have to do is place that particular slip of paper at the head of its column. Otherwise, write your theme on a new slip of paper before placing it at the head of the column. These themes will become the capital letters in point II of your outline — the body — for this essay question. At this stage if you were working on the essay question we are using as an illustration, the table in front of you should look something like this:

Describe the conditions under which the unemployed had to live during the Great Depression.		
No safety net entitling you to help	Available charity	What people did to help themselves
no insured bank accounts	soup kitchens	suicide
no national welfare system	state & local government	selling apples or pencils

no social security	from churches	begging
no unemployment insurance	bread lines	stealing
		riding freight trains

The next step is to arrange the slips within each column in a logical order. When you think you have a good arrangement, write "II. Body of essay" on the first line of a new sheet of paper. Skip a line and indent about an inch and write "A." Tape the theme of your first column right after the "A." On the next line write "1," and tape the first piece of information in that column next to the "1." Go down one more line and write "2" right under the "1." Tape your second item next to the "2," and proceed in exactly the same manner until you have taken care of all the items in the first column. Your sheet from our sample essay with the theme "No safety net" might look like the illustration below:

II. Body of essay
    A. No safety net
        1. no social security
        2. no unemployment insurance
        3. no insured bank accounts
        4. no national welfare system

Do the same thing for the other columns. They will become "B," "C," and so forth. Each should be taped to a separate sheet of paper labeled "II. Body of essay." This way you can easily switch the capital letters around if you decide that the order in which you have them could be improved. The outline of the body of your essay is now complete.

All that is still missing is an introduction and a conclusion. Start a new sheet of paper and tape the question across the top. Skip a line and write "I. Introduction." Skip another line, indent about one inch, write "A.," and follow it with an answer to the question in very broad terms. Skip another line, and write "B. Main points I will cover." Skip another line and write "1." followed by the first theme, which is, of course, item A. under II., the body of your essay. "2." and "3." under that are, naturally items B and C. The purpose of the introduction is to prepare your readers for what you will say, to "tell them what you are going to tell them."

The conclusion will be "III.," written on a separate sheet of paper. The aim of the conclusion is to wrap up your essay by "telling them what you told them." The finished outline of our sample essay question will illustrate what I mean. When you write the essay, the introduction will be one paragraph long, followed by one paragraph for each of the capital letters in the body. The conclusion forms the last paragraph.

SAMPLE OUTLINE

Describe the conditions under which the unemployed had to live during the Great Depression.

I. Introduction
    A. conditions for the unemployed during the Great Depression were terrible
    B. main points I will cover
        1. no safety net
        2. charity that was available
        3. self-help measures

II. Body of essay
    A. no safety net
    B. charity that was available
    C. self-help measures

III. Conclusion
    A. conditions were bad
    B. many had to accept charity due to lack of safety net
    C. available charity not sufficient
    D. self-help measures not enough — many homeless and starving

---

Do each of the essay questions on your study guide or in the chapter review questions in the same way. When you are done organizing the essay questions, give your **don't know** 3x5 cards another run-through before you test yourself to see how well you remember the essays.

Find out how well you remember your essay questions by writing the outline for each of them on a piece of scrap paper from memory. Compare your new outline to the original. If everything is the same, go on to the next essay question. If not, rewrite your outline on scrap paper three times saying the words as you write them in order to use as many senses as possible to etch the outline into your memory. Then try writing the outline from memory again and compare to the original. Keep recycling each essay question in this way until you can reproduce the essay question accurately.

❑ As a final reassurance that you really know the material, find someone to quiz you, or better still, get together with someone else in the same course and quiz each other. Then get a solid night's sleep and a good breakfast. You have prepared well, and can be confident about the test.◆

TakingTests

History tests tend to come in two basic types of questions: objective, and essay. To begin with, reread the test-taking section of chapter I., which describes how to become a savvy test-taker. Be sure to pace yourself, so that you will have time to answer questions that you know the answer to at the end of the test.

Objective Questions

Doing well on objective tests depends on your ability to answer a large number of questions quickly. You either have to recognize the right answer from one or more wrong answers (True-False, multiple-choice, matching), or be able to supply a few right words (fill-in-the-blank, or complete the sentence). In any case, the emphasis is on speed. But you also have to read both the directions and the questions themselves accurately. Missing a double negative in the question or skipping over the fact that the teacher wants to know which item does **not** belong in a series will lead you to lose credit even though you may actually know the answer. As we emphasized earlier, you should gain speed through careful learning of the material and by answering the questions efficiently, **not** by hasty reading.

Essay Questions

Reading is not much of a problem in essay questions, especially if your teacher gave you a study sheet, so that you could prepare all of the possible essay questions ahead of time. In that case, all you have to do is remember your outline and write the essay in good, clear sentences. If you did not get the essay questions ahead of time, your biggest problem is to really answer the question that is asked. The most beautiful answer to a question the teacher **did not ask** will get you zero credit! Unless you get directions to do otherwise, write your answer in good, clear English in complete sentences.

❑ In an unprepared essay it is a good idea to spend a few minutes collecting your thoughts and writing a mini-outline (just the main points you plan to cover). This will keep you from forgetting a major point, keep you on the subject, and may even get you partial credit if you run out of time. In short, mini-outlines help you to be more complete in fewer words and therefore save you time. Your teacher has many papers to grade, and will not appreciate getting a mass of repetitious or unorganized verbiage out of which he or she is supposed to fish the answer!◆

❑ Also, be sure to read the directions carefully, if they state that you should have **at least** a certain number of sentences, be sure to come up with that many without repeating yourself.◆

Conclusion

This chapter has presented a detailed description of the steps required to become a good history student. You have learned that it is efficient to invest the most time and effort on the tasks at the bottom of the pyramid, and to make the tools on each level that will help you on the next level: textbook notes, class notes, etc. In addition, you learned how to go about reading the textbook, how to study for tests, and how to take them. If you put in a lot of daily effort, follow the directions in this chapter, and use your time well, you will see a big improvement in your history grades.

REFERENCES

Baldridge, Kenneth P. *Baldridge Reading Instruction Materials*. Greenwich, CT: 1977.

Pauk, Walter. *How to Study in College*. 2nd ed. Boston: Houghton Mifflin, 1974.

Pauk, Walter. *Successful Scholarship*. Englewood Cliffs, NJ.: Prentice-Hall, 1966.

Robinson, H. Alan. *Teaching Reading, Writing, and Study Strategies: the Content Areas*. 3rd ed. Boston: Allyn and Bacon, 1983.

Thomas, Ellen Lamar and Robinson, H. Alan. *Improving Reading in Every Class*. 3rd. ed. Boston: Allyn & Bacon, 1982.

CHAPTER V

ENGLISH

LITTLE THINGS THAT HELP

1. Do all the "Little Things" from Chapter I.
2. Keep and remember a private list of "power words" to use in your own writing — words you came across in your own reading that made a character or situation come alive for you.
3. Read a little for fun every day.
4. Read novels, short stories, and plays in sittings that are at least thirty minutes long to give yourself time to "get into" the work.
5. If your teacher introduces a new novel, story, or play, pay close attention — the teacher's introduction will help you "get into the story" faster, and understand more.
6. If your teacher has not introduced a new story, novel, or play that you are assigned to read, provide your own introduction by reading a short encyclopedia article on the author and/or the work.
7. Read poems aloud, preferably to another student.
8. Find a partner with whom to exchange themes and other writing assignments for editing — it is much easier to find problems and suggest solutions in other people's work than in your own.
9. Keep an alphabetized list of your commonly misspelled words.
10. Use a word processor, spelling checker, and printer.

Introduction

To achieve as much as possible in life, you have to be able to read, write, and speak well. Communication is the key to success in many careers. English is the language spoken by most Americans and the language of instruction in most American schools. It is the basis for much of the other work you do in school. Later on in the "real world," your skills in English may very well determine the kind of job you will be able to get. It is important to put your best efforts into this subject.

As we have discussed in previous chapters, each subject has its own way of treating language. The way a novelist uses the English language is quite different from the way a scientist or mathematician uses it. The first difference is that the assignments in your English class are much less concentrated than those in other subjects — you may very well have thirty to fifty pages to cover in one night instead of the four or five for your science assignment. (Poetry is the exception to this rule. It may be as concentrated as a math formula.) This means that if you read a novel like a math or science book, it would take you forever to finish. In fact, reading an English assignment very slowly may prevent you from experiencing the full impact of the writing.

A novelist or short story writer uses many different words to get the message across to the reader. This is because literature does not deal with straight-forward, "up-front" types of subject matter. It deals with emotions, feelings, relationships, psychological situations and other things that cannot be described in one word or sentence.

One aim of the novelist or short story writer is to involve the reader in the world of the story. The writer wants you not only to follow the action, but also to feel what the characters feel. In other words, writers want you to "know" about the characters with your heart, not only with your head. As you can see, literature is not an exact science. It **depends** on the reader to be an active participant in the process.

Words are the only tools a writer has to perform the miracle of "getting you inside" the unreal world of the book or story, so that you will treat the plot and the characters as if they were actually real. Writers use words much like painters use colors to create shapes and moods. Because writers deal so much with feelings and other complicated matters, they often describe what they are talking about in a rather indirect manner. The reader in turn has to do a good deal of "reading between the lines," to get the message.

For this reason, the emotional response that a word like "mother" evokes in the reader is often as important as what the word means on the surface. Another problem with words is that many have several different meanings, while others mean just about, but not quite, the same thing; like colors that are close, but not identical.

While words are the building blocks for experiencing and understanding the novel or story, it is the whole work, rather than the individual words, that is important. In fact, the whole process works best if novels and short stories are read at about ten times the speed that you would use for a science book. You should also allow at least thirty minutes for each reading session to give the writer enough time to "hook" you. And do not worry if you skip over some of the words. If the writer really feels that a particular thing is essential for the reader to know, it will be repeated in other words.

Still, understanding literature is not easy. In addition to words that were used four hundred years ago (in reading Shakespeare, for example), you may also be faced with references to the Bible, other literature, history, etc. that may not be part of your own background. And poetry presents its own special difficulties; poets use not only the meaning of words, but also rhythm and sound to get the message across to the reader. In addition, this may be your first contact with grammar.

The other side of reading is writing. It is likely that you will be asked to do a good deal of it in English class, even though you may not have had to do much in school before this. So the task may be new to you. Technology can make writing easier than it used to be, though. Use a word processor if you can. Professional writers would not be without one, because they greatly simplify the editing process. You can add, delete, and switch text around easily.

In addition to being able to change things easily, you do not have to rewrite everything for each new draft — just any words you added. Spelling checkers are another lovely item. They find and correct spelling errors, but since the computer does not know the difference between words you misspell and words you mistype, you can type much faster than you can with a normal typewriter. Mistakes are easy to find and correct. All this encourages you to edit and rewrite to come up with much improved written work.

English, then, is not an easy subject, but the pyramid to good grades applies to English as it does to your other subjects. The rest of this chapter will teach you how to go about doing your work in English class in a structured and organized way.

Pyramid to Good Grades in English

Taking Tests
Read directions and questions carefully. Use techniques of good writing to present information. Answer objective questions on vocabulary and grammar tests.

Studying for Tests
Make up & answer essay questions. Make vocabulary cards. Use quizzing procedure to learn vocab. Review "personal textbook." Redo grammar missed on homework assignments.

Class Work
Participate in discussion of reading assignment. Take notes. Contribute to group work on writing project. Correct grammar exercises. Note new assignment and any teacher explanation.

Homework
Do prereading activities. Note "power words." Read novels, short stories, plays, poems. Use "bare bones" notetaking system. Make "personal grammar textbook." Do grammar exercises. Write themes, short stories, poems.

Homework

The most important level on the pyramid to good grades in English is the same as it is for all other subjects: Homework. It will take the most time and effort, but it is the basis of success for all the other levels. Although homework is often not graded, you will be at a disadvantage in class discussion, writing assignments, and later tests if you have not done a good job on it.

Reading and writing literature is easier if you become familiar with some of the "tools of the trade" — the main devices that authors use to give their writing added impact. The technical terms used to describe these "tools" are listed and defined in the **glossary** at the end of this chapter, so that you can easily refer to them. Your teacher will use these terms in talking about works of literature, so you need to learn them. Incorporate these devices into your own writing and see how much more effective it can become.

Homework in English class usually involves reading and/or writing. Let us start our discussion of how to do English homework by showing you how to do your English reading efficiently. The following section, however, does not apply to reading poetry. Poetry is a very special case and will be discussed later.

Reading a Novel or Short Story

Find a nice, comfortable place where you will not be disturbed, and plan to spend at least thirty minutes in each reading session. You should try to do your English reading all at once, not in little bits and pieces. It usually takes at least this much uninterrupted time for the author's words to work their magic and let you, the reader, leave the real world and enter the world of the story.

Providing yourself with "space" to become part of the story is very important, because literature is a two-way street. In the process of transferring the message from the writer's head to that of the reader, the reader is every bit as important as the writer. The way you react to a short story or novel has much to do with your own background, and past experiences — your input. This means that what you get out of a book or story may be somewhat different from what your neighbor gets out of it.

This becomes important in interpreting the meaning of the novel or story. There will be some obvious "surface" plot lines that everyone will agree on, but many interpretations of the deeper meanings are possible. However, when defending your own interpretation during class discussion, make sure that you can back up your views with clues from the book, in other words, what gave you the idea in the first place.

The more involved with the author and the story you are, the easier and more fun it is to keep on reading. Two tricks to accomplish this are to visualize the story, like a TV show or movie in your head, and to stop at points where the tension is high and try to predict what will happen next. If the author and you are "on the same wavelength" you should have a pretty good idea what is about to happen.

Also keep in mind that literature is meant to be read relatively fast. Do not worry about remembering tiny details; knowing the meaning of every single word is not important. When an author feels that the reader absolutely must understand something, he will repeat the information with somewhat different words. For this reason, too, do not interrupt the flow of your reading to take extensive notes.

Good readers keep up a sort of running conversation with the author. This is easy to accomplish if you get a hold of a copy of the book that you can mark up. Books are meant to be written on and in as part of your role as reader. It is no trouble at all to put a check, a question mark, or brief comment in the margin. You will want to mark such things as unclear items, first descriptions of characters or the setting, and anything you strongly agree or disagree with. This "bare bones" system of taking notes is a way to mark what you want to remember without interrupting your communication with the author. The system is also useful for reminding yourself of important passages for class discussion the next day.

It is also a good idea to underline "power words" as you come across them. To make the reader understand the characters and their world, the author uses many words that call up particularly vivid images. English courses usually include writing, so if you make a list of words and phrases that "worked" to get you inside a story in your role as reader, these same words and phrases should be useful to you when you switch to the role of writer. Before you finish your reading session, add these underlined words and phrases to your list of "power words."

As far as homework is concerned, the important thing is to be prepared for the class discussion, otherwise you will be "out of it" the next day. There will undoubtedly be times when the work bunches up on you, and you just cannot finish the English reading assignment. On such occasions (and they should not happen very often) do not follow your natural inclination and start where you left off the night before. Instead, always do the current homework assignment first. That is what will be discussed in class.

At the earliest opportunity go back and read those parts you skipped. Treat this method as an emergency procedure only; try very hard not to get behind. You miss much of the author's build-up if you read in this way. In addition, the story may be hard to follow.

Prereading

As in the other subjects, you want to set up conditions that will make understanding and remembering what you have read as easy and successful as possible. The more you know about the material being presented, the easier it is to read and understand.

The easiest way to "get into" a piece of literature from the student point of view is, of course, for the teacher to introduce the material. He or she may do this by telling you something about the author, the time in which the story takes place, the setting, or the characters.

This preview helps you to get into the mind of the author, which makes reading the actual words easier; and if you do not have to work so hard reading the words, you can spend more energy on feeling and understanding what the author is trying to tell you. You will also stay interested longer, and, naturally, the more interested you are, the easier it is to stay involved, and the more enjoyable it will be.

If the teacher does not introduce a new story, it is well worth your while to spend about half an hour providing such an introduction for yourself, to help you get past the first few pages and into the story. This is not all that hard to do. If you are unfamiliar with the author, you might look the name up in an encyclopedia. The article might even mention the particular novel or short story in your assignment. Remembering something about the time and country from your history class is useful if the assignment is a historical piece.

You may find the classics, such as the works of Shakespeare, which you are certain to be assigned at some point in your high school career, a little harder to read. They are not about modern situations, and many words may be "archaic," which means written in the English of several hundred years ago.

You will save time and be more successful in the end if you go through a more thorough prereading program for "classic" assignments. Try to find an easy-to-read version of the book or play to get the main idea of the plot and find out something about the characters. For Shakespeare, Richard Chute's *Stories from Shakespeare* is a big help. It is also comforting to know that you can go back to Chute should you lose the thread of the action reading the original Shakespeare.

Next, and this is very important, scan the pages that you plan to read, and underline all the words that you have never heard of. Then look up the words in a comprehensive dictionary or a book like *Brewer's Dictionary of Phrase and Fable*. This extra effort will pay off later, because you will be able to read along much more easily and will not be disturbed or distracted by these unfamiliar words.

Reading a Play

First of all, do the usual prereading activities that are described above under "Reading a Novel or Short Story." If you have followed the suggestions above, you will come to the play with a good deal of background, all of which makes the play more interesting and easier to understand.

Reading plays presents some peculiar problems. As you know, plays are meant to be performed on the stage. So the playwright uses not just words, but also scenery, costumes, and action to get his message across to the viewer. An actor's look or gesture, rather than actual words, may "say all there is to say."

When you read a play you should imagine it performed. In fact your role as reader is like that of the director of the play. To get the full impact, you have to translate the playwright's directions (the stage instructions) in your mind into scenery, costumes, and action. It is a bit like making a movie or video in your head.

Still, playing director does not substitute for an actual stage performance, so the easiest way to "get into" a play is to see it performed. You can probably find some of them on video — ask your librarian. If at all possible, try to see the play before you start to read. This will make it much easier to visualize the action when you read the words.

Each production of a play, indeed, each performance, is a kind of "reading." So, too, is your own reading of the play a "performance," directed by you, and staged according to your own interpretation. Some directors have set Shakespeare's plays in the 1940's, and performed Greek tragedies with modern scenery. Just as with a novel or short story, the person seeing or reading the play brings his own experiences and feelings to the reading or performance. There is no one, "right" interpretation. If you have seen the play performed first, you may find yourself "arguing" with the director, and decide that the playwright had something entirely different in mind. You can compare it with your own "production," seeing how they would differ, and backing up your argument with information from the play itself. This is a good, fun way to get involved and stay involved in your reading.

Remember that the words of a play are meant to be spoken, and it is easier to experience the impact of their "music" if you hear them and do not just see them written on the page. Try to find a quiet place where you will not disturb others and read the play aloud.

Do not pass up the opportunity to learn new "power words," just like you did in the novels and short stories. Underline particularly apt words and phrases as you read and transfer them to your permanent list when you have finished your homework. Of course, if you are reading a play written long ago, such as those by William Shakespeare, who lived in the sixteenth century, many of the words may not be used any more or else are not used in the same way today as they were then. Look these up in a college dictionary. If they are not marked "archaic," you can use them without sounding out of date.

Reading Poetry

As noted above, poetry is a very special kind of literature. It has to be read differently from novels, short stories, or plays. The language of poetry is very compressed; every word counts. In addition, most of the poetry you will read has been written according to specific rules. The structure of a poem includes not only its "music" — the rhythm and rhyming patterns — but also the number of lines, and even syllables, that it contains. Sonnets, for example, always have 14 lines, while haiku poems always have 17 syllables, written in 3 lines of 5, 7, and 5 syllables respectively..

Poetry is literature with many layers. It is not just the surface meaning of the words that counts. Just as important are the moods and feelings that the words arouse in the reader. To achieve this latter effect, poetry uses many images and symbols. Poets often express images with unexpected words.

It takes slow, careful, and repeated readings to understand the various layers of meaning in a poem, so be prepared to read each poem several times to get all of the message. In the first reading, just aim to understand what happens (if anything), determine who or what is doing the action, and establish the setting. Are there people, or objects involved? Where does the poem take place? Is it in the woods, in a tenement house, in someone's mind? As you read the poem for the first time, underline any words you do not know.

In poetry, every word is important, so start the second reading by looking up all of the words you underlined. Then concentrate on the use of images and symbols while keeping the basic message of the poem in mind. Try to feel, see, and hear everything the author describes. Also, watch for words that are not usually used together. (The poet may be trying to get you, the reader, to "look at things" in a different way than you are used to doing.) Think of a poem as a little mystery or a puzzle you are trying to figure out. When you think you know what it is about, go back and make sure everything fits your interpretation. Can you think of other possibilities? Finding meaning in poems is like digging for gold, you have to keep looking until you have exhausted the mine.

After the second reading, you should have a pretty good understanding of what the poem is trying to say. (If you still do not get it, reread the poem again and again.) When you have reached the stage where you have a good grasp of the poem, do the same thing that you did with plays: Read the poem aloud to yourself. Better still, read it to someone else. This helps you to experience the rhythm and music of the words more fully.

Let us use a short poem by P.G. Wodehouse (one that does not take itself too seriously) to illustrate how to interpret a poem:

Caliban at Sunset

I stood with a man
Watching the sun go down.
The air was full of murmurous summer scents
And a brave breeze sang like a bugle

From a sky that smoldered in the west,
A sky crimson, amethyst and gold and sepia
And blue as blue as were the eyes of Helen
When she sat
Gazing from some high tower in Ilium
Upon the Grecian tents darkling below.
And he,
This man who stood beside me,
Gaped like some dull, halfwitted animal
And said,
"I say,
Doesn't that sunset remind you
Of a slice
Of underdone roast beef?"

Reading 1

During your first reading of the poem you will have noticed that the only action is two people watching a sunset; one may be the poet himself and the other a man whom the poet describes as "a man," "this man," and finally as "some dull half-witted animal." A third person, Helen, also appears in the poem. The setting is outdoors.

Most of the words are clear enough. You probably have to underline only the word Caliban in the title, and amethyst, and sepia in line 6 darkling in line 10. You already know from reading the poem that amethyst and sepia are colors.

Reading 2

In checking the dictionary, you found out that Caliban is a character in Shakespeare's *The Tempest* and by extension refers to a "dull half-witted" monster. Knowing this helps you to appreciate what the author is trying to tell you in the poem, as does looking up the exact colors he is referring to with the words amethyst and sepia. An amethyst is a semi-precious purple stone. Sepia refers to the grey-brown-black ink of the octopus. The word darkling is not in the dictionary at all, but if you think about it, you can see that the author is probably referring to the darkening shadows of the tents.

During your second reading, you discover the idea that the poet is describing, which is the different way in which two people appreciate the same event. The poet portrays himself as a sensitive, fine-feeling, cultured fellow. He is able to express his appreciation of the sunset by invoking all sorts of references to nature (murmurous summer scents a many-colored sky, crimson, amethyst and gold and sepia, a brave breeze that sang like a bugle), as well as to classical mythology (Helen of Troy, who is a symbol for all that is beautiful, and the high towers of Ilium, site of the Trojan War). His language is fancy and flowery, using literary turns of phrase, like darkling tents, and a blue as blue as were the eyes of Helen.

Then we get to the second man, who clearly has none of the (somewhat overblown) imagination of the poet. The only image that comes to his mind when he sees the sunset is that it looks like a slice of underdone roast beef. From the poet's perspective, he is a dull-witted boor, unable to express himself in refined, poetic ways.

When you read the poem aloud you can hear the difference between the two men as well. Note the long, languorous lines and pleasant sounds that characterize the poet's version of the sunset, and the way he uses unusual combinations of words, like murmurous summer scents. The lines of the second man are short, and no attempt is made to introduce pleasant sounds; that whole section is in fact very stark and unadorned. The idea is that this dull half-witted animal cannot think poetically like the speaker.

The next question you might ask is, what is "poetic thinking" anyway? This poet seems to have a pompous, overblown way of looking at things, and uses obscure words and references to describe them. The language is pretty, but a bit old-fashioned and self-consciously "literary." On the other hand, "Caliban" employs one simple poetic device, the simile, and manages to conjure up a vivid image of a slice of sandwich meat. His poetic imagination is different from the speaker of the poem, but is it necessarily "dull?"

As you can see, poems can be turned around like three-dimensional objects in your mind, as you try to look at them from different sides in order to find their meaning. Once you feel you have figured it out, check through the poem to make sure that everything fits your interpretation. Poems are written not only to make you "feel," but to make you think as well.

Learning Grammar

If you have not taken a foreign language, this may be your first contact with grammar. The advantage of studying grammar is that you learn how English as a language is structured and the labels for the various parts of speech. This gives you a set of terms to discuss how to improve your own writing. Trudy Aronson, *English Grammar Digest* is a handy reference book.

Grammar exercises are a little like math problems. It saves time in the end and avoids a good deal of frustration if you develop a system for doing this type of homework. First of all, you are going to develop a personal textbook for grammar. Why go to the trouble of making a personal textbook, when all of the information is probably available all neatly printed somewhere? The answer is that you will remember things that you write much more easily than if you have just read them. So think about the task as a memory aid rather than as extra work.

Your personal textbook quickly lets you know everything that you have learned so far about grammar. It is a good idea to label each page with the particular part of speech or grammatical term (for example, "adjectives"), and to put only one item on each page. True, this requires a bit more paper, but you will be able to look back and find the information much more easily. Now follow these steps. Note that step 1 involves your class work, and steps 2 and 3 your homework.

Step 1 - **Note teacher introduction**. Your teacher will probably introduce a new grammatical principle or part of speech in class. Pay close attention, take notes and underline words that illustrate the concept.

Step 2 - ❑ **Check the assignment**. Before starting the homework, look in your assignment book to make sure that you are doing the correct exercises.◆

Step 3 - **Fill in your "personal textbook" page**.
Write in any information your teacher gave you. Then read the explanation in your workbook slowly and carefully. Add any new information to the "personal textbook" page. Then describe the grammatical principle in your own words. Finally, write a sentence of your own, underlining the words that illustrate the concept.

Let us assume you are studying "adjectives." After going through the steps, the page in your notebook on adjectives might look something like the following page:

ADJECTIVES

Teacher: A word that modifies another word makes it more specific. An adjective is a word that modifies a noun or pronoun. Adjectives are usually found in front of the noun or pronoun they modify. Example: The red table is in the room.

Workbook: A series of words in front of a noun present special problems. To determine the part of speech, you have to figure out which word is actually being modified. In the sentence, The slightly <u>blue</u> sweater is on the chair. The word <u>blue</u> tells about sweater and is therefore an adjective. <u>Slightly</u> tells about blue and is therefore *not* an adjective.

In my own words: An adjective is a word that tells you something about a noun or pronoun. An adjective defines a noun or pronoun more clearly. Watch out for a series of words in front of a noun or pronoun. Only those words that refer directly to the noun or pronoun are adjectives.

Sentence: The <u>red</u> flower smells fine.

Step 4 - Do the Exercises.
Slow and careful work will get you finished sooner than rushing. The object of workbook exercises is to give you practice in applying the principle that you are studying. Before doing each exercise, check how it illustrates the principle that you are supposed to learn that day. With the principle clearly in mind, do the exercises.

Step 5 - Proofread your work to catch any silly mistakes.
Then you are done.

Writing Themes

Writing and reading complement each other. Instead of reading someone else's ideas, when you write you are putting your own thoughts down on paper so that someone else can read and understand them.

You will undoubtedly not do as much writing as you do reading, but writing themes, as well as short stories, and poetry are standard assignments in English class. English teachers give such assignments so that you will learn to organize your thoughts and express them in words.

The same things that help you to understand the author when you are the reader, help other people understand what you write. Good organization, transitions between ideas, and good word choice help the reader to "connect" with your thoughts.

As in other aspects of school work, having a plan avoids spending a large amount of time staring into space and getting increasingly frustrated, because you have nothing to show for your efforts. The hardest part of writing themes is knowing how to begin. There is that horrible feeling of sitting there with a blank sheet of paper in front of you, but with nothing you think is important enough to say.

The basic plan is the same with all types of writing. First of all, be sure to leave enough time. It is impossible to do a good job if you begin the night before the assignment is due. Leaving plenty of time gives you the opportunity to produce something you can be proud of. After you have a topic, start by brainstorming the assignment. Follow this by making some sort of outline or organizational design. Then write a rough draft, and correct it. Finish by writing a final draft.

Step 1 - Get a topic.
This is usually assigned by your teacher, so all you have to do here is to make sure you wrote the assignment down correctly in your assignment book and to check this before you start work on your theme to make sure that you are writing the theme that was actually assigned.

Step 2 - Brainstorming
Do not expect to just be able to start writing a coherent theme or poem. That is not the way it usually happens. The very act of writing something — anything — can help you to organize your thoughts. To learn to do this is the reason you got the assignment in the first place. The easiest way to get started is to use what is called "free association."

Write down any and all ideas that come into your head that have even the vaguest connection with the assigned topic. Do not hesitate to write down things that seem out in left field. Let your mind wander around the subject. At this stage nothing is crazy or "off the wall." Stop when you have filled at least a page with such "free association," but if your ideas are flowing, do not stop there.

Step 3 - **Reread the assignment, and look over the result of your brainstorming**.

Copy all the ideas that help answer the question posed in the assignment onto a second piece of paper. Cross out the rest (lightly, so that the ideas are retrievable if they turn out to be relevant after all). Do not throw your first sheet of paper away yet. Sometimes ideas that did not seem useful at this stage turn out to be important later on.

Step 4 - **Combine the second copy of your ideas into a rough outline that makes sense out of the brainstorming ideas.**

Rough is the word here; order and symmetry are not important at this stage. What you are doing is pulling out the major ideas from your second sheet of paper, and compiling a sort of shopping list of main ideas. Write these on a third sheet of paper.

By the way, to make sure that you have not accidentally overlooked an important idea from your first brainstorming list, check your first sheet before finishing your list of main ideas.

Step 5 - **Now you are ready to make a detailed outline that you can actually use to write from.**

In order to makes it as easy as possible for the reader to get your message, a theme has a standard organizational pattern — introduction, body, and conclusion — and your outline should reflect this organizational scheme.

Roman numeral I of your outline is the introduction. The function of the introduction is to get the reader interested and to mentally prepare him or her for what you will say in the body of the theme. A sentence or two is all you need to get the reader's attention. Next, you should briefly give the reader an idea what you are going to be writing about — the main ideas.

Roman numeral II of the outline is the body of the paper. This explains your main ideas in detail. You will want to devote at least one paragraph to each of your main ideas. These should, of course, be expansions of the main ideas mentioned in your introduction.

Finally, in the conclusion (Roman numeral III of the outline), you sum up the main points that you want the reader to remember. The conclusion is very much like the main points presented in the introduction, except that you use other words to "tell them what you told them."

An outline for a theme entitled "The Ideal Teacher," is printed below to show you what such an outline looks like.

I. Introduction
    A. get the reader's attention — How Mrs. Smith handled a difficult situation
    B. main points covered in paper
        1. teaching ability
        2. fair
        3. caring
II. Body
    A. teaching ability
        1. "turns students on" to subject
        2. knows material
        3. can "get material across"
        4. challenges students
    B. fair
        1. has no "favorites"
        2. students get grades they deserve
        3. discipline fair
    C. caring
        1. understands students
        2. students can openly talk to teacher
        3. tries to know students personally
        4. cares what happens to students
        5. provides warm, caring atmosphere in class
III. Conclusion
    A. 3 characteristics of a good teacher
    B. final sentence

Step 6 - **Write a rough draft in pencil using every second line.**

If you have access to a computer, make your life easier by using it. The object at this stage is to turn the outline into connected writing that you can correct as easily as possible in the next draft. It is not the finished product, so do not worry about perfect wording. Even if you know you are not being clear just keep writing. The object of this draft is to express your ideas for yourself.

You should end up with a paragraph for the introduction and conclusion, and a paragraph for each capital letter of the body. Turn each capital letter of the body into a topic sentence. For instance, in our theme on the ideal teacher, your first topic sentence in the body of the paper might be "A basic prerequisite of an ideal teacher is to be really good at teaching students the subject matter at hand." Use the rest of the paragraph to explain the topic sentence. Take a look at your collection of "power words" to see if any of them can be of use in writing this theme. If, for some reason, you find that the order of items in your outline could be improved, or that you left out something important, do not hesitate to change your outline.

❑ If your teacher is willing to go over your rough draft and offer suggestions, do not hesitate to take advantage of the opportunity. Or, if your teacher cannot help you, but does not object to your getting help from a classmate, ask a competent peer in your English class to look over your rough draft. Needless to say, asking your teacher or a classmate to do this an hour before the final draft is due will not do! Be sure to start on your theme as soon as you get the assignment, so that you will be able to finish your rough draft in plenty of time for the teacher to go over it and for you to make any suggested corrections.◆

Step 7 - **Correct the rough draft**.

This step usually takes quite a bit of time to do well. Work on it over a whole day. Having used every second line to write your rough draft really pays off now, because you will have space to do your corrections right on the rough draft, crossing out and adding where needed.

If your teacher or peer went over the rough draft, you need to make the changes he or she suggested and any other improvements you can think of. Be aware that when you change something in one place, you may have to change something somewhere else in order to make it fit. Begin with whatever is easiest for you to do, and go on to the next easier item until you are finished.

If no one looked over your rough draft, you have to look through it on your own. The easiest way is to do this in stages. On the first go-through, concentrate on the ideas. Are they really presented as clearly as possible so that the reader can understand your line of thought without further explanation? You wrote them to be clear to yourself, but will other people understand them too? Do not hesitate to write long explanations of complicated ideas. After all, the more complicated an idea is, the more words you will probably need to make someone else understand it.

In the next go-through, check "mechanics." Make sure that every paragraph has a topic sentence, and that the other sentences explain the topic sentence. Delete any material that does not pertain to the topic sentence. Have you helped the reader move from one idea to the next by putting in transitions? Are all words spelled correctly? (Those of you using a word processor with a spell checker, now is the time to put it to work.) Check your list of words you misspell frequently. Make sure that each of them is spelled correctly. Add the "spelling demons" from this project to your list. The third stage is to polish your work. Read the corrected draft aloud to yourself. Are all the sentences complete? Are the words you used the most effective ones to express your ideas? Stumbling or hesitating or running out of breath during a sentence indicates that something is wrong. See if you can make the sentences read more smoothly.

Step 8 - ❏ **If possible, give your corrected draft to someone else to read.**

Having a partner with whom to trade papers is a big help. It is so much easier to find and correct mistakes made by someone else than ones you make yourself! Ask your partner to tell you about any parts that seem unclear. Consider your partner's suggestions, and if you agree with them correct your draft accordingly. ◆

Step 9 - **Type or write out the final draft.**

To make sure no "typos" have crept into your work, proofread the final draft. And last but not least, **hand it in on time.**

Note: Anything longer than a word or phrase that you use that is not your own idea **must** be acknowledged. See Chapter VII ("Writing a Research Paper" pp.189, 195-197) for a discussion of what needs to be footnoted and how to do it. Otherwise you are committing plagiarism (representing the ideas of others as your own), which can have very serious consequences — even getting you expelled from school.

Writing Short Stories

A short story is a special kind of literature. It is a form of fiction, but unlike a novel in which a whole series of happenings may take place, a short story usually analyzes a single event. It has to have a beginning that arouses the interest of the reader, a middle that describes a conflict and builds up the tension, and an ending where the conflict is resolved.

The best preparation for writing a short story is to read one by a successful author and see how he or she did the job. If you have not been assigned a short story to read, look over a short story by someone like

Ernest Hemingway or William Faulkner, and see how it gets you interested in reading the story in the first place, presents the conflict, builds the tension, and finally resolves the conflict.

When writing a short story of your own, the big problem usually is finding an event that can be written about in the form of a short story. As in the case of writing themes, having a systematic way of going about the writing task is the best way to solve this problem. In fact, the steps involved are the same as you followed in writing a theme. This system will get you started and gives you the basic principles involved in writing a short story. In the process, you might find that the story takes on a life of its own, and that you develop your own method; that is the wonderful part of creativity. However, if you get stuck, come back to this book.

Step 1 - ❑ **Check the assignment to make sure that you are not forgetting an important direction or limitation.**
For example, if the assignment is "life in the city," it will not do to present a story that takes place on a ranch in Oklahoma. ◆

Step 2 - **Brainstorm the project.**
Write on a sheet of paper any ideas that come into your head that have anything to do with the assigned subject. If your teacher did not place limitations on the topic, concentrate on situations, settings, and conflicts with which you are familiar. Pay particular attention to finding a conflict, since conflict and its resolution is one of the characteristics of a short story: no conflict, no short story.

Step 3 - **Look over your brainstorming sheet.**
See if any of the ideas light the spark of inspiration. What you need at this point is a usable idea. Many a good story has been crafted from modest beginnings. Do not wait for the perfect idea; perfection is hard to come by.

When you have an idea to work with, begin with the organization of your story: Write down the setting; provide a brief description of each of the characters (including what they are like before and after the story takes place); jot down the high points of the plot including the conflict, and how it is resolved. The fun part about short stories is that you get to make up characters and situations — you are their creator.

Step 4 - **Now you are ready to start the actual writing.**
Write a rough draft, in pencil, using every second line (as usual), or use a computer if you have access to one. A computer can make writing much easier, because it lets you add, delete and move words around later in the editing stage without having to rewrite everything.

The important thing is to start writing and keep going. That way you will have something to show your teacher and to correct. Start wherever inspiration hits you, and fit the parts together later.

The beginning is often the hardest part to write, so you may want to leave it until later. If you have trouble with it, try starting with the climax of the conflict, because it is the core of a short story. Once this is accomplished, you can work forward and backward from there.

As you write the rough draft, your collection of "power words" will come in handy. You may have noted just the word that will help the reader to enter the world of your story — that will help him or her see, hear, and feel as your characters do. Make ample use of the thesaurus as well. A synonym of a word you know is not quite right may give just the "flavor" you need. And, if it is appropriate (for example if your story involves teenagers), do not hesitate to draw on your own knowledge. The jargon used by your group may be just the thing. Also, the length of your sentences and words can be very effective in creating a mood.

If he or she is willing to look it over, show your teacher the rough draft. Just as in themes, direct teacher-coaching is the best way to learn how to write. Discuss your ideas with your teacher in a constructive fashion, making sure that he or she understands what you are trying to do in the story. Again, if your teacher cannot help you turn to a competent peer.

Step 5 - **Correct the rough draft**.

If your teacher went over the draft, you should have some very concrete suggestions with which to work. Again, you do not have to start at the beginning and go to the end. Think about the teacher's suggestions, and do whatever seems easiest to take care of first, and proceed to the next until you have done everything that your teacher asked you to do. After you have done that, make sure the story still says what you want it to say (remember — it is **your** story), and that it makes logical sense. Another short conference with your teacher might be helpful at this stage.

If you are on your own, follow the same three-stage method that you used for correcting the rough draft of a theme. On the first go-through, concentrate on the central idea and the structure of your story. Does the beginning "grab" the reader? Do the characters and their conflict seem powerful? Is the resolution of the conflict plausible? Have you built in transitions, so that the reader can follow the story? Are there enough "tension spots" to keep the reader interested?

In the next go-through, check "mechanics." Make sure that every word is spelled correctly. Again, a computer spell checker makes things easier. Since short stories often involve dialogue, you need to be careful that all direct speech is properly punctuated and capitalized.

❑ The third stage is to polish your work. Read the corrected draft aloud to yourself. Did you choose words that make your story come alive? From your descriptions, can the reader feel that he or she really knows the characters and understands what "makes them tick?" If you stumble or hesitate during your reading, it is an indication that something is wrong. See if you can make the sentence or paragraph read more smoothly. Does the story come alive for you, too? One magical part of writing is when stories develop a life of their own — like children.◆

Step 6 - ❑ **If possible, give your corrected draft to someone else to read and comment on.**

Carefully consider any corrections suggested by your partner, and follow those you think appropriate. Again, you have the final word — it is your story. Make sure the story still says what you want it to say. ◆

Step 7 - **Type, write, or print the final draft.**

Just to make sure no "typos" have crept into your work, proofread the final draft before handing it in **on time.**

Writing Poetry

Like reading poetry, writing poetry requires very specialized skills. There are several different kinds of poems, and each category (except free verse) has very strict rules. For instance, a Japanese haiku is very short; it expounds on only one thought. A sonnet, on the other hand, has to have fourteen lines, an introduction, a build-up section, and a conclusion.

The purpose of this section is to give you a system for writing poetry. It will not guarantee that you write brilliant poems, but it will help you avoid spending a long time sitting with a blank sheet of paper, or panicking because no thought has come to you.

Step 1 - ❑ **Check your assignment and make sure that you know the rules for the type of poem you are to write.**

(If you can write free verse, you do not have to worry about such stringent rules.) ◆

Step 2 - **Brainstorm the poem.**

Get a blank sheet of paper and a pencil. In a column at the left-hand margin write words as you think of them. At this point you are not trying to come up with anything connected, just trying to get something to start with.

Step 3 - **Now try to think up as many words that rhyme with the words on your list as you can.**

You can also look in a rhyming dictionary to get more ideas. Write each rhyming word on the same line next to the original word. This "rhyming word" technique is useful even if your poem does not have to rhyme. It gives you a large number of words to spur your imagination. When you are finished with this stage, the first few lines of your paper should look like this:

SAMPLE POETRY BRAINSTORMING LIST WITH RHYMING WORDS

debate, rebate
fear, tear, dear
fun, run, sun, pun, gun
day, may, say, way, play, tray, clay
soon, moon, boon, loon
boat, moat, float, coat
duck, luck, truck
fish, dish, wish
rain, plain, train, main, plain
tower, flower, power

Step 4 - **Find an idea that connects at least some of the words on your list.**

Include the rhyming words in your search. This is not as difficult as it sounds at first. One of the peculiar things about our minds is that, if we do not force them to do otherwise, they tend to come up with words that have some connection to each other.

Step 5 - **Write a rough draft of your poem using every second line.**

Try to express the idea that connected your words in the type of poem you were assigned to write. Use as many words as possible that call up vivid images, sounds, smells, and textures, so that the reader uses all of his or her senses to appreciate what you are describing. If you are supposed to use rhyme, the rhyming words should help. Look over the glossary at the end of this chapter to find literary devices that you can use in your poem. For example, it is perfectly appropriate to let an object represent a complicated feeling or idea, such as using flowers as symbols of beauty, castles as symbols of strength, etc.

As in themes and short stories, start as soon as you get the assignment, so that you will have the maximum chance of getting suggestions from other people, especially your teacher. If your teacher is willing to look over your poem, show him or her your rough draft. Discuss your ideas, keeping in mind that you are the author.

Step 6 - Correct your rough draft.

If your teacher made comments and suggestions, think them over, and make the suggested corrections. Start with a suggestion that is easy to incorporate. After you finish that, do the next easiest item and so forth until you have made the changes that your teacher suggested, and that you feel are appropriate. However, if you do not agree with one of your teacher's suggestions, do not hesitate to talk it over with the teacher and argue about it if necessary. You are the author.

If you have to "go it alone," start by reading your poem aloud to yourself, and try to play the role of critical reader. As usual, dividing the task into several go-throughs makes it easier.

The first time through, concentrate on the way the words express your central idea. Listen to the sound and rhythm of the words. Do they allow a reader to "plug into" your emotional wave-length and express your ideas as forcefully as possible? For example, in describing a rock, you might use hard sounding words (if that is the aspect of the rock you are writing about). On the other hand, soft-sounding words would evoke a different "meaning."

In the second reading concentrate on mechanics. Have you met the formal requirements of the type of poem you are to write? Are all words spelled correctly?

The last go-through is to give your poem the final polish. ❑ As in other types of writing, exchanging papers with someone else at this point is very helpful. At the very least, read your poem aloud to someone else. Do not be modest, or afraid to share your work. If you hesitated or had to read something twice, a correction is probably necessary.◆

Step 7 - **Write or type out a clean final draft.**
Proofread it to make sure that there are no typos, and **hand the finished product in on time.**

Classwork

Classwork is the second most important level on the pyramid to good grades. Setting yourself up for doing a good job in class is especially important because you want to learn and remember as much as you can from class discussion. This will help you do well on the inevitable tests and improve your writing skills.

❑ To begin with, it is just as important to get to class on time with your homework well done in your English course as it is in your other courses. If you arrive a few minutes early and get a chance to look over any comments you made on the assigned reading, it will be a big help in getting your mind focused onto English and away from your last class.◆

English classwork usually includes discussion of the assigned reading, or group work on the current writing project as well as getting a new assignment. In any case, you need to be an active participant. The reason, as usual, is that the more engaged you are and the more ideas you contribute on your own, the more you learn and remember. If you sit there passively and let other students and the teacher do all the work, you will learn maybe a quarter of what an active participant learns. And, of course, the following truism applies here as well: What you have not learned you cannot remember. To put it very simply: The more you put into an activity, the more you are likely to get out of it.

If you have done your part by doing a thorough job on the homework, you will have the materials and information you need to interact with the teacher and the rest of the class. You will not be bored, "turn off," and waste the class period.

Reading

If the day's classwork is the discussion of a reading assignment, classwork is your chance to accomplish two goals: to check your own comprehension of the reading and to get a "free" review. You do not have to invest a single minute of "your own" time.

If you are not used to participating fully in class, it takes a good deal of courage at first to volunteer answers to questions and give your ideas on a piece of writing. Just remember, your opinions, when backed by relevant references to the text, are as "right" as anyone else's. One of the nice things about literature (unlike math, science or even history) is that there are seldom absolutely right or wrong answers. Even if you do seem to be "wrong," it is no reason to feel stupid — use the experience to learn how to discuss literature.

As you overcome your reluctance to participate actively in class discussion, you will notice not only that it becomes easier, but also that your views are taken more seriously by the teacher and your classmates. There is no easier and more effective way to get the most learning out of the class period.

Use the class discussion to get any questions you had while you were doing the reading for homework clarified. (Remember the notes you made in the margin.) In addition, check your understanding of the characters and plot as well as the deeper meaning of the work by answering the teacher's questions in your head even when someone else has been called on.

Take notes on the discussion. Your class notes do not have to be a beautiful outline, just brief statements of what the teacher considered important and what was said in class.

These notes will be very valuable when you study for the test; as you know, in English class there is no "end of the chapter review test" to use as a study guide as there is in math class. The class notes you take are a major source of insight into what your teacher considers important, and therefore an excellent guide to what the teacher might ask on the test. Items and interpretations stressed in class are very likely to reappear on the test. In short, the better your class notes are the better your test grade is likely to be.

Writing

If the day's task is group work on a writing assignment, you want to use the class work to get as much advice as possible from the teacher and other class members on your own theme, story, poem, or play. Again, doing a good job on your homework gives you the basis for getting the most out of class.

Listen carefully to any discussion of the basic principles involved in the type of writing you are doing. If you have the opportunity, read what you have written so far aloud to the group and listen carefully to the suggestions made by the teacher or other class members. In this group situation, be assertive, but also be respectful of others. Make the experience work for you and your partners. Take notes on any subsequent discussion and suggestions that apply to your piece.

Do not be intimidated by the clash of egos that sometimes takes place in such group situations, nor let one or two classmates dominate the discussion. To make the class discussion work for you, you need to be assertive, but also respectful of other people's views. It works both ways.

Grammar

If the work of the day is to go over a grammar assignment, you have two tasks during class: First of all, you want to be sure to get anything that is not crystal clear to you cleared up. By the end of class your knowledge of the lesson should be rock solid.

Your second task is to correct the homework exercises. If your teacher lets you, write the correct answer in red (or any other color you did not use for the original work) below or next to your original homework. The purpose in doing this is to provide yourself with a perfect copy of the work you were assigned for homework to use later in studying for the test.

New Assignment

❑ When the teacher gives the new assignment listen carefully and write it in your assignment book. As mentioned in Chapter I, countless student hours are wasted every year in doing the wrong assignment. Do not let that happen to you.◆ If the teacher introduces a new piece of literature, pay attention, because listening carefully to the teacher's introduction means that you can save yourself a whole step in the homework process.

Studying for Tests

Your grade in most English courses is determined by your score on tests and your grades on the various writing assignments. (Writing is covered in the homework section, and so will not be repeated here.) This means that tests do not play as big a role as they do in other classes, but they can still make the difference between a good and a poor grade in the course. English tests usually cover the reading you have done, vocabulary, or grammar.

Studying for a Test on Reading

This is the most common type of English test. Tests on the reading you have done usually take the form of essay questions, and in order to do well on these tests you will need to do two things: 1) Learn the material so that you will be able to recall it under the pressure condition of test time, and 2) organize the material so that you will be able to do a good job presenting it in a convincing fashion. Note: As usual, you want to organize your time, so that you learn the most in the shortest time and spend none of it spinning your wheels.

Step 1 - Finish reading and check the assignment.
Finish any reading that you have not done yet. Then check your assignment sheet to be sure that you study all of the material that will be covered on the test.

Step 2 - Find out what you do not remember.
This is much harder to do for a test on your English reading than for other types of tests. As we saw, there is no "end of the chapter review test," so that you have to structure your review on your own.

Test your memory of what the work was about by writing a description of the plot, a sketch of each of the main characters, and their functions in the plot. After you have done this, look back at your class notes and margin notes as well as the text itself to fill in any missed items — which are really just blanks in your memory. Underline the missed parts, so that you will be able to pay particular attention to these items in the next step of your review.

Now look through all your class notes (your best source of information on what your teacher considers most important about the reading) for possible essay questions. Think of the broad questions your teacher asked. What you are looking for is questions that pull the text together for you. Such questions are good candidates — but probably in slightly altered form — for test questions. You should word your own essay question so that the answer will include all the information discussed in class. Write each question at the top of a separate sheet of paper. If you have done this job

ENGLISH

well, there is not too much that the teacher can surprise you with on test day.

Next, answer each essay question right on its sheet of paper. Making up and answering these essay questions can help you get a good test grade on two fronts. First, they organize and help you remember the material covered in the reading. And secondly, they give you practice in organizing your thoughts and writing good essays. Since you are being graded on how well you present your thoughts as well as on the information presented, do not underestimate the importance of the second factor.

As you write, underline or highlight any material you had to look up. This will indicate where you need to put your efforts in the next review step. It is also a good idea to impose a time limit — ten to fifteen minutes per question.

Step 3 - **Study all your essay questions**.
You are not aiming at memorization; the aim is to get yourself to the point where you can reproduce the ideas in a well-organized, logically convincing form. As you go over the questions, pay special attention to the underlined parts. These are your weak spots.

Step 4 - ❑ **Get a solid night's sleep and eat a good breakfast**.
The teacher is not likely to ask questions just precisely the way you formulated your own essay questions from your class notes, so being in good shape to think will help you to get a good test grade.◆

Studying for a Vocabulary Test

A large, sophisticated vocabulary pays off in a number of ways: it helps you communicate your ideas effectively, and helps you get good grades in your own writing, on vocabulary tests, and on such crucial tests as the SATs and other national or state exams. Vocabulary is a standard section on these "aptitude tests," and improving your vocabulary is one of the best ways to improve your scores.

Luckily, studying for a vocabulary test in English class is not really a problem at all. Since you probably know which words are going to be asked, all you have to do is learn them. (Actually, your vocabulary lists may contain words and phrases, but for the sake of simplicity, we are going to speak only of words.) The techniques for learning vocabulary are the same for English and foreign languages, so the following system will be useful as well for improving your grade in your foreign language course.

Step 1 - ❑ **As usual, check the assignment to make sure you are learning the correct words.◆**

Step 2 - **Make 3x5 vocabulary cards.**
This looks like extra work, but it is not, because if you go about it correctly, you can already learn many of the words just by making the cards. To get the most learning out of the procedure, combine the multisensory learning approach with context clues as you make the cards. What you are doing, is to make as many connections in your mind with the word as possible, any one of which can give you a way to retrieve the word from your memory. Obviously, the more pathways you have built, the more likely it is that you will remember the word when you need it.

Consciously use as many of your senses as possible. To give a strong visual signal, write the vocabulary word clearly using a color coordination system: write nouns and pronouns in red, adjectives in pink (because they modify red nouns and pronouns), verbs in blue, adverbs in purple (because they modify blue verbs as well as adjectives and other adverbs), and all other words in green.

To add the listening component, pronounce the word distinctly and correctly as you write it. It is important to emphasize correct pronunciation in preparing the vocabulary cards, because it will make it easier to incorporate the word into your speaking vocabulary as well as your reading vocabulary; the more ways you can use a word the more it becomes "your own."

The act of writing itself uses your sense of touch. If you can associate the word with a particular smell, you can even put that powerful but underused sense to work for you as well just by thinking of the smell as you write the word. For example, with the word "fragrant" you can think of your favorite flower or perfume.

Now try to link the new word or phrase with other words on your vocabulary list or with ones you already know. If you know the antonym (opposite) or a synonym (same) of the word or phrase, add that information right below the new word labeling it "syn." or "ant."

Write the meaning of the word on the back of the card. Next, try to figure out some connection you might have with the word. Can it be used to describe someone or a situation you know? A character from a book you read? Any connection will do, but the more vivid it is the more easily you will remember the word. Then use the word in a sentence of your own. The sentence should include a reference to the person, situation, or other connection to which you are "tying" the word. For instance, if the word <u>succulent</u> is on your list, you could write a sentence about a beautiful roast, just ready to eat. As you write, picture the roast in your mind so strongly that you can see, feel, smell, and taste it.

This kind of "tie-in" makes it twice as likely that you will remember the vocabulary word. If you cannot think of the vocabulary word, but **can** think of the "tie-in," the vocabulary word often pops into mind.

Step 3 - **Quiz yourself to find out how many words you have learned just in the process of making the cards**.
For each word look at the front of the vocabulary card and try to say the meaning of the word from memory. If you cannot remember it immediately, try to conjure up the "tie-in" you used.

Turn the card over, and if your meaning matches the back of the vocabulary card, put that card in a pile labeled "**know**." If you missed the meaning, the card goes into a "**don't know**" pile. You may be surprised to find that you already know as many as half of the words on your list.

You will most likely be responsible for spelling the words correctly as well as for knowing their meaning. In that case, write each word on a piece of scrap paper in addition to saying it and learning its meaning. If the word is spelled according to the rules, you are in luck. (Should you not have a clear idea of what the vowel rules of English are, see pp. 59–60 of the science chapter for an explanation.) If not, note any spelling peculiarities. Highlight any irregularities, so that they will hit you in the eye each time you review the word. Incidentally, if you are required to spell the words correctly, you should not put the word in the "**know**" pile until you can spell it correctly as well as know its meaning.

Step 4 - **Study all the cards in the "don't know" pile.**
Say each word slowly, clearly, and distinctly. Then turn the card over and read the meaning aloud. Finally, "call up" the "tie-in" as vividly as you possibly can.

Step 5 - **Recycle steps 3 and 4 until the "don't know" pile is gone.**

Step 6 - ❑ **Get a good night's sleep, and eat a solid breakfast so** you will do well on the test.◆

Studying for Tests on Grammar

Studying for grammar tests is just as straight-forward as studying for vocabulary tests.

Step 1 - ❏ **As usual, check your assignment sheet to make sure you are studying the correct assignment.**◆

Step 2 - **Review the material that will be on the test.**
First of all, take your "personal textbook" and slowly read all explanations of the grammatical principles aloud to yourself. Then make up a new sentence of your own illustrating each principle you are supposed to learn. If you cannot think of an appropriate sentence, or if you find that you misused the principle in the sentence you wrote, reread that principle in your "personal textbook."

Step 3 - **Check your knowledge.**
If you followed the directions given earlier in this chapter, you will have corrected any items you missed on the homework in class the next day, so that you have a 100% accurate version of the homework to study from. You do not want to see these answers until you are finished quizzing yourself, so put a check mark in your grammar workbook next to any item you missed on the homework.
Now redo the checked items. Compare the redone items to the corrected homework.

Step 4 - **Recycle steps 2 and 3 for any items you missed in Step 3.**

Step 5 - ❏ **Get a good night's sleep, eat a good breakfast, and wow them in the morning.**◆

Taking Tests

In addition to the general discussion about how to take tests in chapter I, a few hints about how the general principles apply to taking English tests may be helpful. In general, except for vocabulary and grammar tests, there are fewer objective questions than in other courses.

Taking Tests on Reading

As a case in point, tests on reading are made up largely of essay questions. That means that you have to do more than just recognize the right answer; you have to supply the information from your own memory. Your job is to use the information you gained from your own reading and from the class discussion to answer the teacher's questions. There are two criteria that teacher's use in grading essay questions: 1) does the information in the student's essay answer the question asked and 2) how well is the information presented?

Your diligent review for the test should mean that you will have no trouble meeting the first requirement. There is no substitute for doing a good job studying for the test. If you paid attention to your teacher's discussion of the reading, took good class notes, and followed the suggestions in the previous section, you are likely to find that the questions on the test are just variations or parts of the essay questions that you prepared and answered for yourself.

Nevertheless, while knowing a lot about the reading is essential for getting a good grade on a reading test, it is not enough. The easiest way to meet the second criteria — good writing — is to follow the directions for writing a good essay found in the section on homework.

The first paragraph of your essay should briefly state what you will be writing about. (On a test you do not need to worry about getting your teacher interested in reading your essay.) Each of the following paragraphs deals with an aspect of the question. Every part of the question gets a separate paragraph, with a topic sentence and the other sentences explaining the topic sentence. The last paragraph of your essay "tells them what you told them"; it should be a brief restatement of paragraph 1.

You also have to read the questions themselves carefully to make sure that you are supplying the right information and all of it. Teachers frequently write questions with several parts to them. This may look forbidding at first glance, but it actually helps structure your answer by telling you which aspects the teacher wants you to cover. To get a good grade, all of the parts need to be addressed. Use the teacher's question as a structure and write down the major points you want to make before you start writing. This is an easy way to make sure your answer is on target and includes the entire question. Such a mini-outline saves you time and trouble. It will go a long way to keep you from writing on and on, repeating points you have already made, and not including others you should be making. Your teacher has many essays to read, so being asked to pick the appropriate answer out of a mass of unnecessary and irrelevant material does not make a good impression.

When you have finished your essay, read it over to make sure that all of your answer deals directly with the question asked. Large amounts of interesting, but not very relevant information takes much time to write, but probably will not help your grade. You also need to make sure that you answered all of the question. No matter how beautiful your essay is, if it does not answer all of the question it will not deserve a good grade.

Taking Vocabulary and Grammar Tests

We can discuss these two types of tests together, because unlike tests on the reading, they will both be objective tests. Your task in objective tests is to be able to pick the right answer out of a number of options (multiple choice), fill in the blank, or write a sentence or two applying a grammatical principle or using a particular vocabulary word.

Since you knew which vocabulary lists or grammatical principles will be covered on the test (and studied accordingly), there should be no mystery about the actual test questions. And knowing that you have prepared well for the test should help you to take the test in that calm, cool, relaxed manner that is conducive to high grades.

There are usually a fairly large number of questions on an objective test, and your grade is determined by how many you get right. Objective tests put a great deal of pressure on your reading ability. In order to get the correct answer, you have to 1) follow the directions and 2) read and understand the question correctly. As in all tests, answering a question that is not asked should get you no credit.

Speed and accuracy, then, are the watchwords. The way to combine speed and accuracy is to proceed systematically. Begin with accuracy. ❑ Start by reading the directions slowly and carefully. Do not start to answer the questions until you have a very clear idea of what you are to do. If there is any doubt in your mind, ask your teacher to clarify the directions. This is **not** the place to gain speed. Students lose countless credit on objective tests because they either did not read or did not understand the directions.◆

Now proceed at a steady pace, but do not rush your reading of the questions. Remember, you cannot answer a question correctly if you have not read it correctly. If you are not sure, reread the question. Be super careful not to skip over such vital words as **not**. In fact, any question worded in the negative deserves two readings. Underlining the essential words in the question might help you to understand the question.

Then go through the test first answering all the questions you know right off the bat, that you do not even have to think about, first. As you go through the test, put a check mark in the margin in front of any question you did not answer. That way you will not waste any time finding unanswered questions when you return to the items you did not know immediately. When you have answered all the questions that were easy for you, go back and work on the ones you have to think about. When you have answered a question, erase the check mark.

Allow five minutes at the end of the test to look it over for careless mistakes, and to make an educated guess on any questions that still have check marks. The only condition under which it does not pay to guess at this point is when you are penalized more for a wrong answer than a blank. (This is the situation on some tests, so find out ahead of time if there is a penalty for guessing.)

❑ **Never change an answer unless you are positive the new answer is correct.** Statistically your first hunch is more likely to be right, and you will feel terrible if you changed a right answer to a wrong one.◆

Conclusion

In this chapter you learned how to be an efficient English student. We dealt with recycling your learning at each level of the pyramid to good grades and with mastering the things you will need to do a good job on the next level. You learned how to read novels, short stories, and poems; and how to write themes, short stories, and poems.

The homework section was the most detailed, because you should be spending most of your time on the materials that make up homework in English classes: reading and writing, learning new vocabulary and the principles of grammar. Doing a thorough job on your homework prepared you for participating actively in class discussions. Such participation in turn helped you to check your understanding of the homework, as well as providing feedback and ideas from your teacher and fellow classmates on how to interpret the reading or proceed with a writing project.

The short stories and poems you write for English class provide one measure of your learning, but there are also tests to take. This chapter contained suggestions on how to study for reading, vocabulary, and grammar tests. We concluded with hints on taking such tests so that you will get maximum credit and a good grade in the course.

Glossary

Allegory - Using symbolic or figurative language to tell a story.
Example: Like the north star, she guided his path through life.

Alliteration - Repetition of consonant sounds in a series of words (mostly at the beginning of words) — used extensively in poetry.
Example: "The weary, way-worn wanderer" (Poe, "To Helen")

Allusion - Reference to a person or place in terms of a commonplace image that the writer assumes the reader is familiar with.
Example: He has the memory of an elephant.

Anaphora - Repetition of a word or phrase at the beginning of several verses, clauses, or sentences — used extensively in poetry.

Antithesis - Use of words or ideas that are opposites.
Example: Their personalities clashed like night and day.
Circumlocution - An indirect or round-about expression.
Example: "It was decided to streamline the work force in the interest of greater efficiency," instead of "one thousand employees were fired."

Climax - The high point of the action in a play, poem, or story.
Example: The scene in a detective novel when the murderer is exposed

Euphemism - A mild expression substituted for a realistic description of something disagreeable.
Example: "He passed away," instead of "he died."

Hyperbole - An overstatement, an exaggeration.
Example: mile-high buildings

Inversion - A reversal of the natural order of words in a sentence.

Example: "I kid you not."

Irony - Using words to signify the opposite of what they usually express. For example, disguising ridicule as praise.
   Example: "You guys really did an outstanding job," said the coach to his team after it lost the game 38:0.

Metaphor - Treating one object as if it were another object.
Example: "His words were a rushing torrent."

Motivation - The causes that account for the way a character behaves.
   Example: "All his life he wanted to prove he was worthy of his father's trust."

Onomatopoeia - Words, whose sounds suggest their meanings.
   Example: "roar," "clank," "murmur"

Oxymoron - A figure of speech in which contradictory or nonsensical terms are used together.
   Example: "O heavy lightness, serious vanity!"

Parable - A short story that makes a moral point by using comparisons with natural and familiar things. The New Testament of the Bible is full of parables.

Paradox - A statement that is really true, but sounds contradictory or absurd.
   Example: Tea can be a stimulant or a depressant.
Personification - Giving human qualities to abstractions or inanimate objects.
   Example: "The stone rose up and hit me."

Simile - A comparison between two things using like, as, appear or seem.
   Example: "He drinks like a fish."

Symbol - A figure of speech in an object stands for something else at the same time as it is itself.
   Example: A flag is a piece of colored cloth at the same time as it stands for a nation.

This glossary of literary terms was compiled from a variety of sources including: C. Hugh Holman, *A Handbook to Literature*; and Philip McFarland et al., *Themes in American Literature*.

REFERENCES

Aronson, Trudy. *English Grammar Digest*. Englewood Cliffs, NJ: Prentice-Hall, 1984.

Baldridge, Kenneth P. *Baldridge Reading Instruction Materials*. Greenwich, CT: 1977.

Brewer, E. Cobham. *Brewer's Dictionary of Phrase and Fable*. New York: Harper & Row, 1981.

Chute, Richard. *Stories from Shakespeare*. Cleveland: World Publishing Co., 1956.

Grassi, Rosanna and DeBlois, Peter. *Composition and Literature: A Rhetoric for Critical Writing* Englewood Cliffs, NJ: Prentice Hall, 1984.

Holman, C. Hugh. *A Handbook to Literature*. 4th ed. Indianapolis, IN: Bobbs-Merrill, 1980.

McFarland, Philip, Kirschner, Allen, Ferguson, Larry D. and Peckham, Morse. *Themes in American Literature*. Boston: Houghton Mifflin, 1972.

Pauk, Walter. *How to Study in College*. 2nd ed. Boston: Houghton Mifflin, 1974.

Pauk, Walter. *Successful Scholarship*. Englewood Cliffs, NJ.: Prentice-Hall, 1966.

Shaughnessy, Mina P. *Errors and Expectations*. New York: Oxford University Press, 1977.

Thomas, Ellen Lamar and Robinson, H. Alan. *Improving Reading in Every Class*. 3rd. ed. Boston: Allyn & Bacon, 1982.

CHAPTER VI

FOREIGN LANGUAGES

LITTLE THINGS THAT HELP

1. Do all the "Little Things" mentioned in Chapter I.
2. While doing your homework write out two or three questions you can ask in class the next day.
3. Incorporate use of the foreign language into your lifestyle; a pen pal, films, records, books on subjects of special interest to you, and traveling are some examples.
4. If you know any native speakers (parents, grandparents, neighbors), practice speaking the language with them.
5. Review vocabulary you do not know yet during one-minute "quickie reviews" at least twice daily.
6. Answer mentally when classmates recite.
7. Check the library for foreign language tapes and magazines, especially magazines with many photographs with captions.
8. Try "talking to yourself" in the language.

"It's All Foreign to Me..." Tasks and Difficulties in Learning Foreign Languages

This chapter will show you how to develop the skills needed to become a good student of foreign languages. As with all the other subjects, it is not a matter of suddenly becoming smarter. Following the directions in this chapter will help you be better organized and get the most out of the instruction you receive in school. With daily effort and good use of your time, you will see an improvement in your foreign language grades.

Foreign languages have to be approached a little differently than other courses. You are not mastering a body of information, rather, you are learning a new way to communicate. To add to the confusion, ancient foreign languages (mainly Latin in the U.S.) are taught somewhat differently than modern languages. The instruction in Latin stresses vocabulary and grammar to enable you to read and write Latin texts. No one speaks conversational Latin anymore, in fact, nobody is really sure what the language sounded like when spoken by the ancient Romans. Teachers of modern foreign languages, on the other hand, are concerned with listening and speaking as well as with reading and writing. Particular stress is placed on the students' ability to communicate orally.

This means, on the plus side, that you do not have to worry so much about oral communication in Latin. Unfortunately there are some negatives as well: since Latin is taught mostly on the basis of ancient texts, the teachers are likely to insist on having you learn the one right word and precise language structure to reproduce those ancient texts you are reading. In addition, you cannot offset low grammar grades with a good ability to speak the language. Finally, since the topics of the readings are classical too, many have little relevance to life today. As a result, it is harder for students to "get into" what they are reading about.

This problem of irrelevance to your life may bother you in learning a modern foreign language as well, but it is much easier to overcome. In the first place, chances are you have chosen a particular language to study because you were interested in it for some reason. Also, in a very real sense, today's world is a "global village." Films, records, books, magazines, and various cultural events are often presented in foreign languages, particularly in major cities that have large immigrant populations. You should certainly try to take advantage of such events. (Shaughnesy, p. 125)

If in the course of attending foreign language "events" you make friends with people speaking "your" foreign language, so much the better. That would give you a chance to practice speaking the language outside the school environment, and make it all that much more fun. Understanding and making yourself understood in a foreign language is a real thrill, and once you experience it, you will be even more motivated in your studies.

In addition to learning a new way to communicate, there is another built-in problem: This may be your first contact with grammar. Not knowing English grammar is a serious handicap in learning any foreign language in school; with the heavy emphasis on translating and grammar, students of Latin have an even harder time than students of modern foreign languages.

FOREIGN LANGUAGE

Fortunately, there is help available for just this sort of problem. The *English Grammar Digest* is a quick review of English grammar. In addition, there are relatively inexpensive paperbacks geared for each specific foreign language, for example, *English Grammar for Students of French*. (See the at the end of this chapter for publication references data.)

The familiar pyramid to good grades (on the next page) applies to foreign languages just as it does to your other subjects. For this reason this chapter is also organized around these levels; they are the bold print subdivisions. (The introduction and conclusion, are not part of the pyramid.)

The way to proceed is to read the chapter through first to get an overall idea how to go about being a good foreign language student. Apply the "Little Things" right away to get quick results. Then work through the chapter. Apply the information in each level to your own foreign language course. Start by doing your next homework assignment following the suggestions in this chapter. Expect the first sessions to take a bit longer than you usually spend on homework — any new method takes longer at first. You will be rewarded for your efforts, however, by showing up in class the next day very much more prepared. That will in turn encourage you to study and apply the classwork, review, and evaluation levels. Good luck.

Homework

Learning another language, ancient or modern, is something that requires a good deal of daily effort. The process is very cumulative: In other words, you never forget any of the vocabulary or grammar that has been presented, since all later material is based on the earlier lessons, and is fair game for tests and quizzes forever after. You can never say, "well, the test is over, so I do not have to worry about this material any more!" You are learning a new system of communication — to be a master of the language you must master **all** its elements.

Languages are complicated, and the more practice you get using your new communication tool outside of the classroom the better. The "Easy Things" list at the beginning of the chapter includes some of the ways to build use of the language (especially if it is a modern one) into your lifestyle, so that you can bring your receptive (reading and listening) vocab-

Pyramid to Good Grades in Foreign Languages

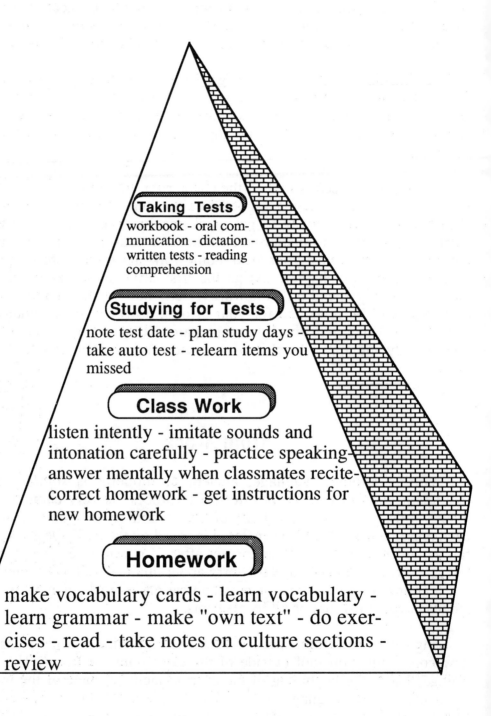

Taking Tests
workbook - oral communication - dictation - written tests - reading comprehension

Studying for Tests
note test date - plan study days - take auto test - relearn items you missed

Class Work
listen intently - imitate sounds and intonation carefully - practice speaking - answer mentally when classmates recite - correct homework - get instructions for new homework

Homework
make vocabulary cards - learn vocabulary - learn grammar - make "own text" - do exercises - read - take notes on culture sections - review

ulary into your expressive vocabulary (speaking, writing). You do not have to do everything every day, and you might be able to think of other avenues of providing yourself with informal, "fun" use of the language. The more pleasant the ways of practice and association, the more likely you are to do them.

The "normal" learning tasks of any class — doing your homework and reviewing regularly — are especially important in foreign language courses. Fortunately, the rewards are also great. You will be using all the vocabulary and grammar throughout your foreign language "career," so the earlier you learn it, the less time you have to spend looking up the words and rules that you need to have at your fingertips in order to do the current assignment. Similarly, being prepared right along means that you can participate actively in the oral work that goes on during class.

A good study environment (discussed in chapter I) is naturally important, as it is with all subjects, but foreign language study has an additional requirement. If possible, you need a place where you can study aloud without embarrassment. "Quality time" for doing your foreign language homework is also important. Try to arrange half-hour chunks in which you can give the foreign language your absolute, undivided attention.

As in your other subjects, most of your homework will be based on textbook assignments, so it is well worth your while early in the semester to survey the textbook and find out how it is set up and what helps it contains. Most foreign language textbooks have an English-foreign language and foreign language-English dictionary, an index, maps, and a summary of the grammatical forms presented in that textbook. Some will contain such additional aids as lists of irregular verbs and glossaries that will point you to the lesson in which words or phrases were first introduced.

As in your other subjects, doing your homework according to a plan saves you time. Do not rush in to do the assigned exercises before you learn the material on which the exercises are based. This will save you a lot of time looking up words and grammatical points. For both classical and modern foreign languages, do your homework in the order below. You might make a copy of the list and put it in front of the foreign language section of your class notebook, so that you can refer to it when you do your foreign language homework.

1- Check your assignment sheet to make sure that you are doing the correct assignment.

2- Learn your new vocabulary by making vocabulary cards and mastering the words and phrases.

3- Learn the new grammar and make your "own text" entry.

4- Do the exercises.

5- Read any passages assigned.

6- Read and take notes on the culture section if any (these are usually written in   English).

7- Review.

Check the Assignment

This step is the same for all subjects: ❑ Check your assignment sheet. Do not waste time and effort doing the wrong assignment!◆

Learn Your New Vocabulary

The basis of mastering a foreign language is learning vocabulary, and unfortunately, this is often difficult and can be boring. The trick to making it easier is to employ the same techniques that you use to learn formulas for science. The vocabulary you have to learn usually falls into three categories: words and phrases that you learn easily, a middle group that takes a little extra work, and a hard core that takes a great deal of recycling and effort on your part to master. The trick to memorizing is to give each group just the amount of attention and effort. The first group — the easy words — you can learn almost "for free" in the process of making vocabulary cards.

Make Vocabulary Cards

When making the 3x5 vocabulary cards, you want to incorporate two powerful "tricks" that make remembering easier: 1) use a multi-sensory approach to learning the material and 2) link the new word or phrase to as many words that you already know as possible. With the first technique you are bombarding your brain with information using several pathways: speaking, and writing, obviously, but also seeing, hearing, and even tasting if you can figure out a way to do it, so that the new information makes a strong impression. The stronger the impression, the easier it is to recall the material later. The second technique uses the principle that it is easier to remember connected items and especially ones that you can tie in with what you already know.

Write the foreign word or phrase clearly on the front of the card to give a strong visual signal. Include accent marks, articles, irregular forms, and/or principal parts, just as the word is given in your textbook vocabulary. Maximize your learning by color-coding the vocabulary words by part of speech: nouns or pronouns in <u>red</u>, verbs in <u>blue</u>, adjectives in <u>pink</u>, adverbs in <u>green</u>, other parts of speech in <u>black</u>.

Try to link the new word or phrase with other words in your assignment or with ones you already know. Write an adjective you already know (properly colored pink) in front or in back of each noun or pronoun as is proper for "your" language. Put an adverb (green) next to every verb, and noun (red) you know next to each new adjective. This action automatically gives you the gender of nouns, links the new learning to what you already know, and gives you another avenue to recall the new word. If you know the antonym (opposite) or a synonym (same) of the word or phrase, add that information right below the new vocabulary labeling it "syn." or "anton." If the word you are studying is a verb, list its principal parts above the verb and adverb. Also note anything that is irregular about your word on the bottom of the foreign language side.

As you write the new vocabulary, pronounce the words distinctly and correctly using the pronunciation rules your teacher taught you. This adds the listening component. It is important to emphasize correct pronunciation in preparing the vocabulary cards, because getting your ear accustomed to the language is really critical. As you can imagine, getting used to the sound of another language is an especially important key to understanding it. It is tremendously helpful to memorize the alphabet as recited in the foreign language. Try to spell out the words in your head, using the foreign pronunciation of the letters.

On the back of the card write the English translation of the word or phrase in ballpoint, so it is easy to see which side of the card is up. Here, too, add the translation of any synonyms or antonyms (properly labeled "syn." or "anton." If you are good at drawing, use your talents and supplement the written translation with a picture of the thing or concept represented by the vocabulary word or phrase. Even if you are not an artist, you can use symbols or stick drawings for many words (for example left ←, right →, up ↑ ,down ▼ . If your visual memory is any good at all, pictures are much easier to remember than written words, and the drawings may help you relate to the foreign word directly without translating it into English — a big plus in teaching you to think in the foreign language.

A model vocabulary card for the French word <u>table</u> is shown below.

SAMPLE FRONT OF 3X5 VOCABULARY CARD

le (black) grand (pink) table (red)

linked words:la (black) petite (pink) chaise (red)

SAMPLE BACK OF 3X5 VOCABULARY CARD

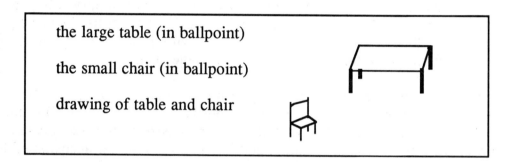

the large table (in ballpoint)

the small chair (in ballpoint)

drawing of table and chair

Making vocabulary cards may sound like extra work, but it really is not, because you not only have an excellent memorizing tool at your disposal, but **may have already learned about a quarter to half the words on your list just by making the cards.** The next step — in order not to do more work than necessary — is to find out which words or phrases you have, indeed, already learned by going through the quizzing procedure.

Quizzing Procedure

❑ Look at the English side of your vocabulary cards and try to say the foreign language words as you write them on a sheet of scratch paper. Turn the card over, and if your translation matches the front of the vocabulary card 100% (including accent marks if any), put that card in a pile labeled "**know**." These are the words and phrases that belong to group 1, the vocabulary that you learned "for free." If your translation does not match the front of the card, it goes into a "**don't know**" pile. These cards need the intensive and more time-consuming treatment of the memorizing procedure.◆

Memorizing Procedure

❑ Take each of the cards in the "**don't know**" pile in turn and look first at the foreign language side. Say each word and the words you have linked with it slowly and accurately several times, and concentrate hard on picturing the word in "your mind's eye" for five seconds after each time you say the word. If you can think of something meaningful to pair this word or phrase with, it will make the word or phrase much easier to remember. Spend another few moments picturing the object or situation described by the foreign language word or phrase and the pairing item. The more vivid the picture is in your mind's eye (with colors, taste, smell, etc.) the easier it is to remember. Then turn the card over and concentrate on etching the English meaning into your memory. Proceed through all the "**don't know**" cards in this fashion. Then work on the "**don't know**" cards the other way around — English to foreign language.◆

Finally, to find out which of the words and phrases you have studied can be switched from the "**don't know**" to the "**know**" pile, repeat the quizzing procedure above with these words. Your "**don't know**" pile should be a good deal smaller now. It would be nice to keep recycling this procedure until your entire "**don't know**" pile has disappeared, but stopping when you know three fourths of the words or phrases is more efficient. You will go through the memorizing and quizzing procedures with this third group, the hardcore words, again in your various reviews.

Learn Grammar

Start learning the grammar of your foreign language homework by reading over your assignment sheet, including any explanation the teacher gave in making this assignment. Look in your textbook to find out what the point of grammar in this lesson is, and read the entry in *English Grammar for Students of* ... if you do not know the English grammar equivalent.

Read the textbook's explanation of the new grammatical points slowly and carefully. Give yourself a mental "hook" on which to hang the new information by relating it to what you already know. How is the new rule or form the same? How is it different from English? Is it the same and different from the foreign language rules and forms you already know?

Often the new grammatical points consist of forms, as, for example, verb forms for the various tenses. Here, the quickest way to learn is memorization, but, again, with a multi-sensory twist. For example, you can give yourself extra visual input by writing the forms in your favorite bright color. Highlight the parts of the word that change by framing them in yellow to make the subject of the lesson especially clear.

MODEL VERB FORM DIAGRAM

(the present tense of French regular "er" verbs)

je regarde	nous regard**ons**
tu regarde**s**	vous regard**ez**
il regarde	ils regard**ent**

Note: The yellow highlighting is indicated with bold print.

With the textbook example in front of you, adapt the diagram above to your own lesson. Clearly write each form on scratch paper five times. Each time, say the word with extra emphasis on the parts that change. This procedure gives you strong visual, oral, and even kinesthetic (from writing) in-put. Each time you write out the diagram, try to go as far as you can without looking at the textbook. Then check your version against the textbook. Whenever you make a mistake, correct your own work; cross out any form that is wrong and write the correct one next to it.

If the new grammatical point introduced is a rule, write it out on scrap paper five times with the model from the textbook in front of you. Say the rule aloud as you write to increase your multi-sensory input.

It is often difficult to remember the exact wording of textbook explanations of grammatical rules. This is not actually necessary. In fact, if you can put the rule into your own words, you can prove to yourself that you really understand it. Lay the textbook aside and write the rule in your own words on a sheet of scrap paper. If you cannot do it, or if your version is wrong when you compare it to the textbook, go back and restudy the textbook explanation until you can do it.

Write "Own Text" Entry

In order to facilitate quick reviews of grammar concepts and to help you firmly fix the lesson in your mind **before** you start on the exercises, write your own personal version of each grammar lesson in your "Own Text." Clearly label the grammatical point that you have been assigned across the top of a piece of notebook paper (for example: **agreement of nouns and adjectives**). Rewrite the rule in your own words. Below the statement of the rule illustrate its use in an easy sentence of your own. Highlight the words that illustrate the rule in yellow.

SAMPLE "OWN TEXT" ENTRY

Agreement of Nouns and Adjectives

Rule: An adjective must agree with the noun or pronoun it tells you something about in number, and in gender.

Sentence: J'ai des petits pois dans mon assiette. (The words "petits" and "pois" should be framed or highlighted in yellow.)

If the grammar lesson involves forms, again start by writing what the lesson was about (such as **present tense**) on the top line. Then make your "Own Text" entry: a 100% correct copy of the diagram you used to memorize the forms — yellow framing and all. Again, write an easy sentence of your own illustrating the use of the form. The collection of your "Own Text" pages, which you should store in your class notebook, will give you a mini-textbook readily available for various reviews.

Do the Exercises

You are now all set to do the assigned exercises. The time that you spent (twenty minutes or so) making the vocabulary cards, memorizing the vocabulary, learning the forms, and making your "Own Text" entry will certainly make doing this part of your homework faster and easier, and much less frustrating.

First of all, be sure to continue the multi-sensory approach as you do the exercises: Say the words or phrases in the exercises aloud clearly and accurately as you write them. Pronouncing the words helps you in two ways: 1) it increases the sensory input and therefore aids your memory, and 2) the combination of hearing and seeing the language over and over reinforces the relationship of letters and sounds in the foreign language, something you need to know in order to write in that language.

Spread your "Own Textbook" entry and the vocabulary cards in the **"don't know"** pile out on your desk so you can easily refer to them if you get stuck, but try to get as far as you can without looking at them. If you have trouble with a sentence or word in the exercises, write as much as you can, leaving blanks for the words or letters you do not know. Look at your cards or "Own Text" to fill in the blanks. If these sources of information that you have readily at hand do not take care of your problem, look in the textbook to fill in any remaining blanks.

Reading

Part or all of your assignment may consist of reading a foreign language passage, so here are some tips on how to learn to read most effectively. What you are aiming for is to be able to read the foreign language in the way you read English, which means getting the meaning directly from the written word without needing to translate it in your head.

As you did when you learned to read English, begin by reading aloud. Do not make the transition to silent reading until you can read aloud pretty well. In addition, again as in English, the more you know of what the writing is about, the easier it is to comprehend the author's meaning.

With this in mind follow the steps below to make your reading as easy as possible. In Latin, a word for word translation is usually required. But here, too, following the steps helps you do a better and faster job. First, read the entire passage fairly quickly to get a general idea what it is all about. Do not stop to look up any words you do not know or try to puzzle out strange constructions.

Second, go back over the passage this time reading carefully. Try to get the essential point of each sentence without making a complete translation. Read to the end of the sentence before looking up any words or constructions. Even if there are unfamiliar words, the context of the words in the sentence may tell you what they have to be. Each language has its own patterns (the order of words in a sentence and words that tend to be used together) and when you have internalized these patterns you can use them to figure out the meanings of words you do not know. If the sentence still makes no sense after you have used all the clues you could get from the sentence and the passage, you do have to look up any unknown words.

Finally, if your assignment calls for it, translate each sentence as you finish it. With Latin, it might make translating easier, if you write the English words above the Latin ones (provided the book is yours) as you puzzle out each sentence. In modern languages, however, where an idea for idea, rather than a word for word, translation is usually called for, using the "write above" system might actually hinder your understanding of the ideas in the foreign language.

If you are not asked to translate the passage, write a summary in English so you will remember what it was all about. If you can do it, write your summary in the foreign language. Note that both the translation and the summary come after you have already understood the author's message in the language in which it was written. Put the translation or summary into your class notebook.

Culture Section

If a culture section is included in your homework, read it carefully and take brief notes. This material is usually presented in English, so it should not take you long to read. Do not skip these sections, because the information is very likely to show up on the next test. Put your notes in your class notebook as well.

Review

❑ As usual, you are not quite finished yet. When the homework assignment is done, briefly review the grammar and vocabulary to fix the day's work in your mind. The five minutes you spend doing this will greatly increase the amount of material you remember tomorrow.◆

Vocabulary

You will be working with your "**don't know**" pile of vocabulary cards. First see if you can switch any "**don't know**" cards to the "**know**" pile by going through the Quizzing Procedure (p. 160) again. By this time, that pile should be down to a few words that are really hard for you to learn. Fasten the "**know**" and "**don't know**" cards with rubber bands, and put them with your class notebook.

Grammar

Give yourself a fast run-down of the day's grammar, by trying to write the rule or forms from memory on a sheet of scratch paper. If you cannot remember the rule or forms reread the "own text" entry.

Class Work

As noted in earlier chapters, class work is important in all courses, but it has an extra dimension in modern language courses. Unless your school has a language lab, class may be the only place where you will find out how to pronounce the words of the foreign language correctly. (This is obviously less of a factor for ancient languages, although here, too, hearing the word gives you an additional sensory input that will make learning easier.) Textbooks, no matter how they try to explain sounds, cannot do justice to the oral part. For this as well as all other reasons mentioned so often in this book, it is very much worth your while to come to class on time, ready and able to participate fully.

"Get Into" the Foreign Language

❑ Use the five minutes before the beginning of class to help you "get into" the foreign language. The more mentally involved you are in the language, the easier it is to think of words and understand them in that language. So, use this psychological fact to your advantage by talking to the teacher or your fellow students in the foreign language before class begins. If this is not possible, at least try "talking to yourself" in the language, perhaps describing what a classmate is wearing. Doing this gets your mind in gear for the class. The idea here is to open up the special foreign language compartment in your brain.◆

Classroom Behavior

When you start to learn a modern foreign language, learning to hear and pronounce new sounds is a basic requirement. Since you do not know how the language sounds or which sounds are associated with what words and ideas, you need all the concentration and cues you can get to understand and reproduce the new sounds and words. This requires a higher level of listening than is true for most of your other classes. Extraneous noise, which might not bother you in classes that are conducted in English, will be very distracting. Quiet and concentration in the foreign language classroom are essential, and you should do everything you can to achieve this. It is certainly in your interest — the teacher already knows the language. It is the students who suffer if the classroom atmosphere is less than optimal.

The ideal way of mastering a foreign language is to learn to think in that language. Right from the beginning, try to associate words and phrases with the objects and ideas they represent directly, rather than attempting to translate the foreign language words into English words. Always listen for meaning, not just words. You will know that your study of the foreign language is beginning to "take" on that special day when you know the foreign words for something that you are trying to say, but cannot for the life of you think of the English version.

It is much easier to understand someone else who is speaking in a foreign language than it is to speak yourself, but the only way to learn is by doing. And much as you learn to hit a baseball by batting the ball around on the practice field, so class participation is the practice ground for speaking the foreign language. Do not be afraid to try to participate; answer questions, take part in role playing or read aloud. Everyone makes mistakes; errors are simply a chance to learn how to do it right.

Besides practice in speaking, you get two other benefits if you actively participate in class — you get review without having to spend any study time, and you receive feedback (without being graded) on what you know and what you have not yet mastered. Without this feedback, you will not know what you do **not know** until test time, when it is too late to do anything about it. If you just sit there in class, you hardly get the most out of your time.

It is true, of course, that in a class of twenty or more students, no single student gets a chance to answer very frequently. But there is a way to participate 100% of the time. You can get around the fact that you will not be center-stage very often. ❏ Get extra review, practice, and feedback by giving the answers mentally, which a classmate has been asked to give "publicly." Similarly, if a classmate is asked to read a passage, read along silently, pronouncing the words mentally. See if you can correct the reader's mistakes before the teacher does.◆ A student often "tunes out" when he or she is not called on — a serious waste of class time in any course, but particularly so in modern foreign languages. Learn to stay "tuned in."

Another way to get the benefits of participation is to listen and respond to foreign language tapes. The only disadvantage is that the tapes are not correlated to your lessons, and you will not get as much direct payoff with improved scores as you will by super class participation. So use tapes for added practice, not as a substitute for class participation.

Homework

At some point in the course of the period, your class will undoubtedly go over the homework that was assigned the day before. Again, pay super attention. If your teacher lets you do it, correct your errors in a color that you are not using for anything else, so that you will have a perfect version to keep in your notebook for upcoming reviews.

If you do not know why your own answer was wrong, ask your teacher to explain it. This is no time to be shy, or to worry about other people knowing that you made a mistake. It is smart to get the matter cleared up now — that way you will get it right on the test.

The teacher will also give new homework. Write the assignment down carefully on your assignment sheet along with any special instructions, explanations, or illustrations the teacher may give you.

Summary

The two watchwords for classwork in foreign language courses are **concentrate** and **participate**. Use your foreign language class as a practice field to master an art that is useful in other courses as well: intense concentration and 100% participation. At all times "tune in" and answer mentally when other students recite.

Review

In foreign languages the payoff for regular, spaced, periodic review is even greater than it is for most other subjects. Foreign languages, like mathematics, are extremely cumulative: each new grammar and vocabulary lesson assumes that you know and will keep using whatever material came before. This puts a premium on conscientious reviewing. Reviews at the end of your homework and quickie reviews should become a daily thing for you; you should not need the threat of a quiz or test.

If you really learn everything well as you go along, it leaves you free to concentrate wholly on new material as it is presented and you will not have to spend time frantically looking up vocabulary and/or grammar with which you should already be familiar. Keeping up, then, saves time and cuts down on frustration.

This is a good time to stress again that you get the most payoff by putting in time and effort regularly every day. "Recycling" of material is a standard feature of foreign language instruction, so the sooner you learn the material, the longer you can use it. And each time you use it, the material is reviewed and reinforced.

We have already discussed the review that should take place right after you finish the homework assignment. In addition, doing a "quickie review" at least twice a day can greatly increase your retention. (Thomas and Robinson, p. 185) Such "quickies" mean spending (literally) a minute or two of odd time such as when you are getting dressed, or going to school to read over the vocabulary in the "**don't know**" pile, five words that are already in the "**know**" pile, or doing a rapid run-down of a grammatical form or tense. With almost no effort at all, you will remember much more and save a good deal of time as well.

Review Before Quizzes

Teachers give quizzes to test whether or not students are keeping up with their daily work. Quizzes are much shorter and less formal than tests, and they involve very specific bits of knowledge. It might be the vocabulary for the day, but it might also be oral work, or written answers to oral questions.

If you have done a good job on the homework and reviews, you do not need to do anything special for quizzes. You will be prepared for a quiz whenever the teacher springs one on you. A very nice payoff.

Review Before Tests

Doing your homework thoroughly and reviewing periodically will not only mean an easier time on quizzes; studying for tests, too, will take less time, and the results will be much better than if you had not worked as efficiently. The rewards of daily effort are now coming in.

❑ As in all other courses, the first step in studying for a foreign language test is to be absolutely clear about what material will be covered. Many a student has forgotten to study for an assigned test, and many more have studied the wrong material. How frustrating, and what a waste of effort! Be sure to write down test dates on your assignment sheet immediately when the teacher announces a test and note any extra directions the teacher gives you. Then mark the days that you should be reviewing for the test on your assignment sheet, and actually study for the test on the days you have marked.◆

If your textbook has auto-tests, follow the routine below. (If your textbook does not have such an aid skip to p.171.

Step 1 – Take the auto-test without looking at the textbook, or your "Own Text." Correct the auto-test and mark the items that you missed for any reason, including carelessness.

The reason for taking the auto-test without any preparation is to find out what you know and what you do not know, so that you can put in "quality time," studying what you are having difficulty with, rather than wasting time relearning what you already know.

Divide the errors you made on the auto-test into vocabulary and grammar mistakes by circling words missed because you did not remember them and putting a red X next to a mistake you made because you did not remember the grammatical rule or form.

Step 2 – Relearn the vocabulary you missed using the vocabulary cards you made while doing your homework. Pull the card for every vocabulary word or phrase circled on the auto-test. Look first in the **"don't know"** pile; that is where these words probably are.

Use these 3x5 cards to do the **memorizing procedure**, and **quizzing procedure** sequence familiar to you from doing your homework the usual five times. Since all the vocabulary covered on the test may not be included in the auto-test, go through the **quizzing, memorizing, quizzing** procedures five times with the cards still left in the **"don't know"** pile in your drawer.

Step 3 – Now start with the errors on the auto-test that involve grammar rules or forms. (These are the items you marked with a red X.) Figure out which points of grammar they are (for example, agreement of adjective and noun), and make a list on a piece of scratch paper, so that you can cross out the points after you have learned them. Taking one grammar mistake at a time, go over the "Own Text" entry that covers each of your errors. Go through the usual learning routine: Write each rule or diagram five times, pronouncing each word carefully as you write it.

Retake the grammar items you missed on the auto-test. Cross out the point on your scratch pad if you have done the item correctly. Repeat the learning procedure and retaking of the items until you can do them all correctly.

Step 4 – Review your notes on all the "culture sections" covered on the test.

Step 5 – ❏ Get a good night's sleep, and have a good breakfast.◆

If your textbook does not have auto-tests, you have to structure your own review, but this is not all that difficult. Just as the people who have auto-tests do, you have to find out what you remember and what you need to relearn of the vocabulary and grammar, as well as cover "culture sections."

Step 1 – Start with the vocabulary. Go back into your drawer and pull out the "**don't know**" vocabulary cards. These are the hard core of troublesome words. Use these cards to do the familiar **memorizing procedure, quizzing procedure** sequence (pp. 160–161) the usual five times. The words that are still in the "**don't know**" pile are super hard -core ones for you. Everyone has some words they seemingly cannot remember. Do not panic, just use this little "**don't know**" pile for further "quickie reviews" at odd moments from now until test time.

Step 2 – For the grammar part of the review, get out your old homework papers again. Figure out which points of grammar you had difficulty with when doing the homework. Copy these (for example, agreement of adjectives and nouns) onto a piece of scratch paper, so you can cross out the rules and forms as you relearn them. (Keep your homework papers in the order in which you wrote down the grammar points or forms you had difficulty with, so that you will not waste time searching for a particular item later on in your review.)

Taking one grammar mistake at a time, go over your "Own Text" entry that covers each of your errors. Go through the usual learning routine: Write each rule or diagram five times, pronouncing each word carefully as you write it.

Find the homework paper(s) on which that particular rule or form was covered. Now use your textbook to redo the item without looking at the corrected homework.

Check your accuracy by comparing your work with the corrected homework. Cross out each rule or form that is correct on the scratch paper. Repeat the learning procedure and retaking of items until you can do them correctly.

Step 3 – Read over the notes you made on the culture sections.

Step 4 – ❏ Get a good night's sleep, and eat a good breakfast.◆

Tests and Other Forms of Evaluation

Tests

As in most of your courses, progress in foreign languages is evaluated through regular, written tests. The steps you should follow in taking these tests are essentially the same as for tests in other subjects. Being well rested, getting to class in plenty of time, with the proper equipment, and only the proper equipment, are all important for foreign language tests. These actions, coupled with the good preparation you did for the test, will help you to do your best. Whether the language is ancient or modern, what the teacher is looking for is improvement in your ability to handle the vocabulary and the grammar of the language.

In applying the good test-taking techniques you learned in Chapter I, start by ❏ **reading the directions** extremely carefully. Do not assume that the directions for one test are just like those the same teacher used in the past. Many students lose much credit because they do not answer the question the teacher asked or else answered it in a way the teacher did not want them to. ◆

❏ Next, you should look over the test and make yourself a time plan, so that you will not spend too much time on the beginning and have no time left for the end of the test. Figuring from the beginning of the test, write the time that you should start on each new section of the test in pencil right on the test. Be sure to leave five minutes at the end to look over the finished test and fill in items you did not know originally. (You are, of course, wearing a watch, if there is no clock in the classroom, so that you can pace yourself.)◆

As in other subjects, careful and thorough preparation goes a long way in providing that calm, cool, and collected state of mind that is so helpful in getting good test grades. If you have done a good job on the review you should be able to proceed through the test carefully and deliberately. Do not rush, but do not spend too much time trying to remember what does not come to you right off the bat. Remember to keep to your time table.

If there are questions the teacher gives you orally and for which you have to write the answer, write the questions on the back of the test as you hear them. This maneuver helps you fix the questions themselves in your mind, so that you will not forget to answer parts of them. In addition, it makes post-test analysis of any errors easy, since it tells your teacher what you thought she or he had said.

When you are dealing with sentences you have to translate or transform by changing elements and you do not know the whole sentence or all the forms that are asked for, write down what you **do** know. Leave room to write in the words you do not know if they come to you later. If you know part of a word, but not all of it, again, write down everything you know and leave dashes to mark the spaces for the letters you do not know.

With this method you might get partial credit for some of the words you did not know completely, and it has the added advantage of keeping you going through the test. You are not spending too much time trying to recall items at the beginning of the test and finding yourself out of time before you can write down items you know at the end of the test. Finally, if you have time to go back to the incomplete items, you are not faced with absolute blanks. What you already have down may trigger recall of the missing parts. Put a check mark in pencil in front of any word or sentence that you did not complete and finish the rest of the section.

❑ If you have any time left when you get to the end of the section, go back and try to improve the checked items. Erase the check mark in front of any item you have corrected. One word of caution: **Never change an answer if you are not 100% sure that the new version is correct**; statistically, your first impulse is more likely to be right, and you will really kick yourself if you change a correct answer to an incorrect one!◆

In the last five minutes, go back and try to correct as many of the remaining checked items as possible. Then look over the whole test. Remember not to change any answers unless you are sure the new answer is correct.

Workbook

If you have a workbook, filling it in is probably part of your homework requirements, but you may also have to turn the workbook in occasionally for evaluation. This should be a chance for you to get a good grade with no extra effort. Check your assignment sheet before you start, so that you are working on the correct pages. Now proceed in the same way as you usually do when doing your homework.

Ability to Communicate

In modern foreign language courses, you will be tested not only on your progress in mastering grammar and vocabulary in written form, but also on your ability to communicate orally. This is a different, although related skill. Obviously, if you do not know a certain amount of vocabulary and are not familiar with the grammatical structure of the language, you cannot use the language to communicate.

The biggest difficulty in speaking is that it takes place within a certain time frame. You cannot ask your listener to stay attentive while you look up a word or grammatical form. But there are advantages as well: in oral communication you can use some aids that are not available when you write or read a language. Speakers can use body language to help get their point across; that puzzled look on the face of the listener alerts a speaker to his or her failure to communicate and tells him or her to try to say the same thing in another way. Remember that at the beginning, the point of oral communication is **to use the language**, not to be elegant or perfect. Learning a language requires a great deal of practice and repetition. You did not learn to speak English in a day either. What counts is the courage to speak. You can strengthen this by private (untested) practice at home using tapes, or, even better, by speaking the language.

What the teacher is looking for in evaluating your oral communication is your ability to transfer thoughts from your head to that of a listener through the medium of spoken words and sentences. The best preparation for this type of evaluation is to be an active participant in classwork. In fact, part of the evaluation of your oral communication may be how well, or at least how often, you participate in class. Keep trying to answer, even if you are not 100% sure you are right.

Your teacher may even test your oral communicative ability by calling you on the telephone. This is harder than face-to-face communication, because you cannot see the teacher's body language and he or she will not be able to see yours. If you know that you are going to be evaluated on your ability to carry on a telephone conversation, practice ahead of time with a classmate. Before the fateful call from your teacher comes, call each other at least five times and carry on a conversation entirely in the foreign language. Do not worry about long pauses or groping for the correct word. If you cannot find the word you are looking for, practice finding other ways of saying what is on your mind. It is interesting and even amusing to notice the different ways there are to express something. You may find yourself taking longer to express a simple idea, even creating "poetic" constructions. This is part of the fun of learning a language.

Dictation

As a student of a modern foreign language, you will probably be faced with a form of evaluation that is not used much in your other classes: dictation. This essentially involves your teacher's pronouncing words or sentences that you are then expected to write down.

Look upon it as a test of your spelling ability in the foreign language. Doing well on dictation requires transferring the sounds of the foreign language into writing. The vast majority of words are spelled according to the phonetic rules of the language, so learning the sound-symbol relationship in the foreign language right from the start is the biggest help you can give yourself.

Learning to spell your vocabulary words will also help you with those words that are not spelled according to the rules. (In no language are **all** the words spelled according to the rules.) Your teacher will undoubtedly concentrate on the words, phrases and sentences you have already studied. This means that doing your homework carefully makes keeping up with the pace of the dictation much easier.

If you are going to keep up with the dictation, you do not have much time to think about what to write, so if you do not know a word or sentence, be sure to put down as much as you know, leave space for the missing words or parts of words, and put a pencil check mark in front of any incomplete sentence or word. Another aid: Sentences should make sense — make sure you have a subject and a verb. If you have a few minutes at the end of the dictation try to fill in the missing parts.

There are two important skills, which you can practice ahead of time, that will help you to do well on dictation: the ability to distinguish the sounds of the foreign language, and the ability to spell the words. Your classroom or language lab may be the only place(s) where you can hear the foreign language spoken correctly, so it is essential that you listen extra carefully in class and or lab.

Another good preparation is the way you go about doing your homework. Saying each vocabulary word as you write it while making out your vocabulary cards and studying the words not only helps you remember the words, but also gets you used to making the transfer between the sound and the written symbols.

Students who think they are making their lives easier by using English spelling and pronunciation for the foreign language words as they learn them will actually be penalized, because they have real difficulty during dictation. Do not fall into that trap. The more you think and function in the foreign language that you are studying, the easier any testing situation will be for you. In fact, as for other forms of testing, the best preparation for dictation is to do a good job on the homework and regular reviews, which is what you should be doing anyway.

Reading Comprehension

Especially after the first year in the modern foreign languages, you will probably have to do some reading of longer passages as part of a test. You will also be asked to answer questions on the reading to show that you understand what you have read. ❑ Be sure to read the directions carefully, so that you know precisely what you are being asked to do. For example, be certain whether the answers are to be in English or in the foreign language. ◆

On a test of reading comprehension use the same system you used when you did reading for homework. Read the passage through quickly first, to get a general idea what the passage is about. In other words, try to read for ideas and not a word-for-word translation. Do not stop to puzzle out any words you do not know. Next, read the questions, so that you can gear your reading to finding the answers.

Then give the passage a second, more careful reading. This time when you come to a word you do not know, try to get the meaning through context. But do not overdo it. Do not linger too long on any one sentence.

After all, you may not even need to understand this particular sentence to answer the questions.

When you find the answer to a question, stop and write your answer. (Put a little pencil mark on the test so that you can find your place again in a hurry.) You may be able to use some of the words and sentence constructions in the passage itself to answer the questions. It is perfectly legitimate to use that kind of help.

When you have answered all the questions you can by this method, reread the questions that you have not answered yet, and look for the answers. If you have time, proofread your answers for spelling and grammatical errors.

Conclusion

In this chapter you have learned how to apply good study methods in your foreign language course. We made a special point of stressing the difference in instructional goals between foreign language instruction and that in other courses. The overall object of foreign language instruction is to improve your linguistic competence. The first time that you can really make yourself understood to a native speaker is a terrifically exciting experience. It makes the hard work worthwhile.

In modern foreign languages you are asked to become competent in all four modes of communication: reading, writing, speaking, and listening. In the last two forms of communication, the classroom is especially important. Much like the lab in science courses, this is the place to get the practice you need for oral communication.

It will be much easier for you to gain mastery in a foreign language if you build use of that language into your lifestyle through reading, talking with native speakers, listening to records and tapes, and seeing movies. Fluency is something that may take years to acquire, but getting a good start now will put you well on your way toward an ability you will treasure for the rest of your life.

REFERENCES

Aronson, Trudy. *English Grammar Digest.* Englewood Cliffs, NJ: Prentice-Hall, 1984.

Goldman, Norma and Szymanski, Ladisla. *English Grammar for Students of Latin.* Jacqueline Morton, ed. Ann Arbor, MI: Olivia and Hill, 1983.

Morton, Jacqueline. *English Grammar for Students of French.* Ann Arbor, MI: Olivia and Hill, 1979.

Pauk, Walter. *How to Study in College.* 2nd ed. Boston: Houghton Mifflin, 1974.

Pauk, Walter. *Successful Scholarship.* Englewood Cliffs, NJ.: Prentice-Hall, 1966.

Shaughnessy, Mina P. *Errors and Expectations.* New York: Oxford University Press, 1977.

Spinelli, Emily. *English Grammar for Students of Spanish.* Jacqueline Morton, ed. Ann Arbor, MI: Olivia and Hill, 1980.

Thomas, Ellen Lamar and Robinson, H. Alan. *Improving Reading in Every Class.* 3rd. ed. Boston: Allyn & Bacon, 1982.

CHAPTER VII

WRITING A RESEARCH PAPER

Introduction

There is no easy way to write a research paper, but there are ways to save time and effort and end up with a better paper as well. The most obvious time and effort saving device is, of course, a word processor. One word of warning: if you are going to use a word processor to write your research paper, learn how to use the machine and the software **before** you are even assigned the paper if at all possible. That will let you concentrate 100% on your research paper when the time comes, and not add the frustration of mastering new technology at the same time.

Writing a research paper involves three consecutive operations: choosing a topic, researching the topic (including note-taking), and writing the paper. This chapter provides a structure (adapted from Kate L. Turabian, *Student's Guide for Writing College Papers*) to guide you through the three parts of the process. Give yourself more time than you think you will need all during the process. Doing a good job takes a lot of time and you do not want to get marked down for turning your paper in late. Remember Murphy's Third Law: If anything can go wrong, it will, and at the worst possible time. To avoid losing any of your cards or papers, buy a big (8 1/2 x 11 inch) manila envelope and keep your cards and papers in it.

If your teacher assigns a topic, the first part of writing a research paper has been done for you. All you need to do now is dash to the library and get the best books and articles, before someone else takes them all out. Then you can go straight to the section on doing your research (p. 183).

Choosing a Topic - What to do and What to Avoid

If your teacher lets you choose your own topic, it is worth your while to spend time and thought on this initial stage, because the topic you choose will have a lot to do with how easy or hard it will be to research and write your paper. There are essentially three situations that arise when the teacher does not specify the topic: 1) the teacher provides limits and these limits fall within the subject matter you have already studied, 2) you have not yet studied the subject matter within the limits of the assignment, and 3) the teacher provides no guidance or limits. You need to read the teacher's instructions carefully to decide which situation fits your individual case. We are going to treat each one in turn.

The first case would arise if the teacher assigned a paper on Shakespearian sonnets and you have been studying these for weeks now. The first thing to do in this case is to get out all of the notes you took on the general subject area. Read through them, and pick an aspect of the subject that interests you more than the rest. Now reread your instructions to make sure that the topic you picked really does fall within the limits specified by the teacher. If so, you know what you can write about in your research paper. Write it down; put the paper in the manila envelope, and get your teacher's OK.

In the second case your history teacher assigns a research paper on any topic you want; but it must fall within the time period 1914-1960, and you have not gotten beyond 1900 in class; this is situation number two. You do not yet have notes on the subject, so the way to proceed is to brainstorm. Dredge up from your memory anything that touches the least bit on the assigned subject area. Have you studied anything in another course that touches on the subject? Look ahead in your textbook, or look at the table of contents of a general book falling within the limits of your assignment. When you have a page worth of thoughts, read through them and pick one aspect or combination of aspects that interests you more than the rest. Now reread the teacher's instructions to make sure that your idea actually falls within the limits. If it does, write it down, put the paper in the manila envelope, and get your teacher's OK.

The way to proceed when the teacher has given you absolutely no guidance is to read through all the notes you have taken for the course up to this point. Choose a topic that interests you more than the rest. If you can tie it in with something covered in another class, you might come up with a particularly interesting and unusual topic. Write down the topic you have chosen, put the paper in the manila envelope, and get your teacher's OK before going on to the research stage.

If you have followed these suggestions and have still not found a topic, you may have to take one that you are less thrilled about. It is easier to research and write about a topic that interests you than something you do not care that much about, but do not spend weeks trying to find the perfect topic. The trick is to find a topic that is neither too broad to cover well in the number of pages allowed, nor so specialized that you cannot say anything useful about it.

In any case, make sure to write down the topic you have chosen, put the paper in the manila envelope, and get your teacher's OK before going on to the research stage.

Research and Taking Notes

Preliminary Research
In the Library — Play "Investigative Reporter"

After choosing a topic your next problem is to find sources of information about it. The best topic in the world is no good, if you cannot find enough information on it. The librarian is your biggest ally in this search. Most librarians are happy to see you use the facilities and delighted to help students, if they are asked in a nice way. If your first encounter is with a sourpuss, do not get discouraged — she may have had a bad day (librarians are people too). Go to another librarian for help. Libraries are there to be used, and librarians are there to help you to use the facilities.

The availability of source material is probably the single greatest limiting factor in doing high school research papers. Many school libraries have only a few books on any one subject. If you have access to a city or college library, it will increase your choice of books, articles, records, pictures, and maybe even movies and videos. Just make sure that you can read the sources you choose. Remember, if you cannot understand a source, it will not help you in your research.

Go to the library with the topic you have chosen, your teacher's instructions, and this book to help you. Start by looking in the subject catalogue or, in larger libraries, ask the reference attendant to help you with a computer search of your topic. Either method will tell you where books on your subject are located. Write down the call numbers of the sources you find. Now go to the stacks and browse. Books on the shelves around the one you originally looked for may be helpful.

List the book (or books) that can serve as sources for your topic. Write down the call number, author, title, place of publication, publisher, and date of publication. Include the library you found the book in (you may be visiting more than one in the course of your research). In the rare case that you have so many sources, that you have to choose which ones to use, give preference to the most recent (the date of publication is listed on the back of the title page), as well as books or articles by famous authors.

If you make yourself a source sheet like the one below ahead of time, you will save time when you get to the library, and you are less likely to omit any of the needed information. You need to repeat this template at least five times for books, so you might want to make copies at the copy machine.

SOURCE SHEET FOR BOOKS

Library:	Call number:
Author:	
Title:	
Place of Publication:	
Publisher:	Date of publication:

For articles go to the *Readers' Guide to Periodical Literature* and check under the general subject that includes your topic. Write down all potential sources relevant to your topic. (If you do not yet know how to use the *Readers' Guide*, ask the librarian to show you.) For articles you need to list the library, the author, title of the article, and the number, volume, and date, and page numbers of the journal. Fill in all the information you can (library and call number must wait for a later stage) on a source sheet for articles like the one on the next page. You will have to repeat the template at least ten times for articles, and again, you may wish to use the copy machine to do this.

SOURCE SHEET FOR ARTICLES

```
Library:                                    Call number:

Author:

Title (in quotes):

Name of journal:

Number:                    Volume:              Date:

Page numbers of article:
```

Check in the card catalog of the specific library you are in to find out if it has the journals. (The *Reader's Guide* indexes articles in many periodicals, but most libraries will subscribe to only a few.) If your library does not have many journals, you might save time and effort by asking the librarian what journals the library has for your topic. Write the call numbers for any journals you find. If this library does not have the journal, note in the margin in pencil "not in — library." Then ask the librarian if she knows of other libraries that have that journal. If your library has an inter-library loan arrangement, the librarian may be able to get the journal(s) for you from another library.

In looking for possible sources, you should also look beyond the obvious ones, like books and articles. Research does not have to be just reading. In fact, some of the most interesting papers result when students use their imaginations and get information from interviews, movies, videos, pictures, or records. (One student went directly to the source and interviewed prisoners and guards in a maximum security prison for a paper on the prison system.) Embassies and consulates of foreign countries, and various trade organizations and labor unions may also have something to offer. The reference librarian can help locate the names, addresses, and/or telephone numbers of such organizations. The more original you are, the more fun your investigation is likely to be. Just make sure to footnote these correctly and add them to the bibliography.

Now it is time to take stock. Ideally, you should have at least four to five potential sources of information for a five to ten page paper. If you have that many different (and accessible!) sources for your topic, borrow or reserve the material. Now make a topic and source sheet to show your teacher for a preliminary OK. Write the topic at the top of a sheet of paper and the sources you have found for it underneath. **Do not throw out your original source sheets with the call numbers and libraries on them,** you will still need this information.

This first stage of writing a research paper will probably not take you more than a few hours to do, however, it is very important **not to procrastinate** at this point. The first people who hit the library have the greatest choice of easily available sources. Do not let the "A" students beat you to the library. The longer you wait, the harder you have to work. If your teacher says "no" to your topic, do not get upset! Start by talking it over with your teacher and determining where the problem is. Sometimes when teachers and students put their heads together, they come up with new sources of information or alter the topic in some way as to make it acceptable. If all this does not result in your teacher's OK, return the books and go back to your brainstorming paper and find your next favorite topic. Go through the search for sources as you did for the first topic you had in mind, make another topic and source sheet, and again show it to your teacher.

On the other hand, your teacher may very well say that your topic is OK in general, but that it is much too broad to be covered in the number of pages that you were assigned, or so narrow that it is hard to say anything very interesting.

Narrowing or Expanding the Topic

Students frequently choose topics that are too broad for the allotted number of pages, so narrowing down the topic to manageable proportions is an important skill. An easy way to go about narrowing your topic is to look at the table of contents and the index of the books you got out of the library, and to skim the articles you have listed on your topic and source sheet for ideas. Reading an article on the subject in an encyclopedia can also help you slim down your topic. If your topic is too large, consider doing a particular aspect of the broad topic (such as a specific event), or a shorter time span. If, on the other hand, your teacher says your topic is too small, choose more aspects, enlarge the time span, or compare your original topic to something relevant.

Cutting down your topic may have the negative effect of cutting out some of your sources, so that you need to find more. This is really a time, effort and ingenuity problem. There are bound to be sources somewhere, but you may not have the time to look for them or have access to the libraries that contain them. Go to another library. Ask your teacher and librarian to help you with ideas. Go back to the card catalog in the library. Try to think of sources other than books and articles, like those mentioned on p. 181. If your library has the books you need, but another student has checked them out, consider asking that person to let you use the books for a day or so one at a time. This stage calls for detective work. Figure out what you need to know, and how you can get this information. Then go out and get it. Be imaginative and persistent. Do not give up.

Developing a Hypothesis

A hypothesis (or controlling idea, as it is sometimes called) is what makes a research paper different from a book report or a simple listing of events. It is a statement in which you are taking a particular point of view, or making a case for a particular interpretation. A hypothesis is a statement, usually in one sentence, that you think you can prove is true on the basis of your research. (Theoretically proving something is false is just as good, but it is harder to do and usually less interesting, so, in general, stick to proving something is true.) The subject of your topic is the subject of the sentence that states your hypothesis. (An example of a hypothesis might be: The election of Abraham Lincoln as president led to the outbreak of the Civil War.)

In formulating a hypothesis, it is also important to keep three "do nots" in mind.

1) Do not try to prove something that is already a well-known fact (for example, "George Washington was the first U.S. president).

2) Do not try to prove an absurdity (for example, "Once a month the moon falls on the earth").

3) Do not try to prove something that cannot be proved one way or the other (for example, "George Washington's false teeth led to the rise of American orthodontry").

A hypothesis not only makes your paper more interesting, but **it saves you a lot of time and trouble**. It guides you in making your preliminary outline and it gives a basic structure to your paper. As a result, you will only have to read things that contribute to proving your hypothesis. You will probably only have to read a chapter here and some

WRITING A RESEARCH PAPER   185 pages there, seldom all of any book. Write down your hypothesis and keep it in front of you as you proceed through the rest of your project.

(Incidentally, if in the course of your reading you come across some information that seems to disprove your hypothesis, do not just ignore it, or discard the hypothesis right away. You have to decide either that this particular author is wrong or, if you think he really has a point, to modify your hypothesis to take account of the new information. You could also state that author's view and disagree with it in your paper, the important thing is to be honest and acknowledge that there is a difference of opinion.)

Making a Preliminary Outline

Take your hypothesis and write down the points that you think you will need in order to prove your hypothesis. Decide which method is a particularly logical way of organizing the information in order to establish cause and effect of your hypothesis. (One point for each assigned page should be about right.) Some ways of doing this are:

1- in order of time
2- from the general to the particular
3- from the particular to the general

A well-written research paper also has an introduction, and a conclusion. In the introduction, you get the reader interested in reading your paper by giving brief background information, stating your hypothesis, and the main points you will use to prove it. The conclusion should be a restatement of your hypothesis in other words and a summary of how you proved it.

Main Point Cards

It is terribly easy at this stage of doing a research paper to spend hours and hours doing research, and still end up having little information that will help you prove your hypothesis. Make **Main Point Cards** to keep yourself organized and looking specifically for information you need and not waste time and energy on information that may be interesting, but not helpful for this particular project.

Write each point (including the introduction, but not the conclusion —

no new information is presented in the conclusion) in ink on the front of a 4x6 card. Number all points in the order you will need them to prove your hypothesis. Next look at the table of contents and the indexes of books as well as the titles of the articles on your topic and source sheet. Decide which source is likely to give you the information you need for each point. In the case of books, also note the page numbers. Look on your source sheet for interviews and other sources that are not books or articles. List this information on the back of each Main Point Card, again in ink, so that it will not smudge. A sample Main Point Card is shown below.

SAMPLE MAIN POINT CARD

Front (point)	Back (sources)
Slave-holding states's views on slavery and states's rights	Standish, Slavery pp. 1-17, 46-62, 75-81 Jones, Slavery pp. 26-42, 34-47, 77-85

The Main Point Cards are very handy, they will not only guide your research, but will also help you make your final outline. If the back of any of your cards is blank, it indicates that you need to look for information on this point while researching other points, and should ask questions about it in any interview you may be conducting.

You will probably list the same sources on several Main Point Cards. This does not mean that you have to read these sources more than once. Just look out for information and take notes on several points at the same time. Also, if you come across information on a point that you are not researching at the moment, do not disregard it, but write down the information.

Letters and Interviews

Now is the time to write any letters requesting information from embassies, trade associations, political parties, unions or other organizations. It usually takes some time to get replies from such sources and waiting for the answers may delay you later on. Also make arrangements for any interviews you plan to carry out.

If possible, do the actual interviewing after you have already done some research; you will be able to ask much more knowledgeable and sophisticated questions. Remember, you are hoping to get from the interviewee what you cannot find out from books and articles, or clarification where the information available to you is not clear. If you are planning to interview some people, keep a sheet with the name of each person you are going to interview written across the top at your side as you read. When you think of questions that person could possibly answer, jot them down on the sheet of paper. If you wait to think up questions until just before the interview, chances are you will forget to ask something that is really important. If the person you are interviewing does not object, record the interview on tape, so that any quotations you use in your paper will be 100% accurate.

The "Real" Research

Now turn to your books and articles. Start with any book or article on your Main Point Cards. Step 1 is to make out a 3x5 bibliography card following the model below. The information you need on the bibliography card is largely the same information that you already have on your source sheets; all you have to add is the short form.

SAMPLE BIBLIOGRAPHY CARD (3X5)

```
Jones, James
 "The Election of 1860"
The American Historical Review,
vol. 84 (spring, 1987) 441-56

Short form: Jones, "Election"
```

Be sure to make out a bibliography card as soon as you are certain you will use the book or article. If you wait until later, you may forget to do it, resulting in a mad scramble for the correct information when you write your bibliography for the finished paper. Keep all bibliography cards fastened together with a rubber band in the manila envelope.

Next you are ready to go on to the heart of doing research: reading and taking notes. You may ask, "Why take notes, it just slows down my reading?" Yes, it does slow down your initial reading, but in the long run making a record of the important points of what you read will save you time. First of all, putting the information you need on note cards keeps you from having to go back to reread your sources when you start to write your paper. Second, following the directions below lets you remember your information (and its location). Third, you will find it easy to organize your information, and you will have all the information you need for your footnotes or endnotes readily at hand.

Students often find taking notes difficult, and it may take some practice to get into the habit. Use cards rather than sheets of paper to take notes, because cards are easy to shuffle and rearrange, and always use all the same size cards to avoid losing the smaller ones. The most useful size is probably 4x6, because you can easily tell them apart from 3x5 bibliography cards, and they are large enough to fit most items of information on one side.

Use only one side of each card. This method takes more cards, but it makes organizing your material later much easier, because all the information will be visible at first glance. If you need two cards for one bit of information, staple them to each other, and number them. Hold all your cards together with a rubber band and put them into your manila envelope.

Write only one piece of information per card, again following the model below. Put down the information in your own words unless you think this is an item that would make a good quotation in your paper. In that case indicate that these are the author's exact words by putting quotation marks around the actual text. If you follow this plan, you will not accidentally quote the author's words in your paper without indicating that this is not your own work. That would be considered plagiarism, which is defined as claiming someone else's "intellectual property," (in this case, writing) as your own work. Plagiarism is a serious offense and some schools will dismiss any students caught doing it, so avoid such temptations right from the beginning. (Incidentally, in case of doubt whether to paraphrase or quote exactly, use the exact quote; you can always paraphrase it later. But it's virtually impossible the other way around.)

On the other hand, you do not want to quote everything exactly, just particularly "quotable quotes." Why go to the extra time and trouble of putting the information into your own words? It's easier in the long run. You do not have to write as much if you condense the information. In addition, you do not have to spend the time putting the information into your own words when you are writing your rough draft.

SAMPLE NOTE CARD (4X6)

main point	main point number	source:author's last name, title short form
	information	
	page number	

Be sure to include all the information on the sample card on all of your note cards. Why go to all that trouble? As usual, including all the information saves you time and effort later. Writing the short form of the source on the card obviously takes less time and effort than the whole citation, but still lets you keep track of where you found the information.

The source and the page number(s) are absolutely essential for the footnotes or endnotes, in which you will have to indicate where you got all direct quotes and information that is not obvious. For example, you do not need a foot or endnote for the fact that the Civil War pitted the North against the South, but you do need one if you say the South was very upset at the election of Lincoln. You do not want to waste precious time while writing your paper going back and searching for the page from which you got your information. Spending thirty seconds writing the information down while taking the note is easier.

When you have finished reading and taking notes on the relevant pages in the sources listed on your Main Point Card, check off the item. This action is not only a reward, but also an easy way to keep track of the progress of your research: how much you have completed and what you still need to do.

Organize your finished note cards once a week according to the numbers on your Main Point Cards. Keep the cards in piles with the Main Point Card on top. Fasten them with rubber bands. You need to determine which main points need further research. This keeps you from spending too much time on points on which you already have enough information. Many students accumulate too much information on some points and then run out of time before they can get enough information on others. Stop working on points on which you have enough information to prove this aspect of your hypothesis when further sources provide little new information.

If there are still points for which you have no or not enough information after you have researched the sources on your Main Point Cards, go back to the indexes and table of contents of your books again. Also skim through the articles, and consider some additional "non-traditional sources" like interviews or films.

If all of this is not enough, go back to the library and search the subject catalog again. Now that you have done some research on your topic, you may think of additional categories to look up. Put your new sources and page numbers on the source sheet.

After you have filled in the "empty" items on your Main Point Cards with the new sources, resume reading and taking notes. When you have enough information on all points to prove your hypotheses, stop your research and prepare your outline. The research itself will probably take you at least two weeks depending on the time you actually devote to research, how fast you read, and how efficient you are in taking notes.

Organizing The 4x6 Cards — Scholarly Solitaire

Arrange your 4x6 cards on a large table or desk. Now play solitaire with your note cards by placing the Main Point Cards in order horizontally across the edge of the table farthest away from you, like the aces in solitaire games). Place all the note cards pertaining to each point in a vertical row underneath like the illustration below.

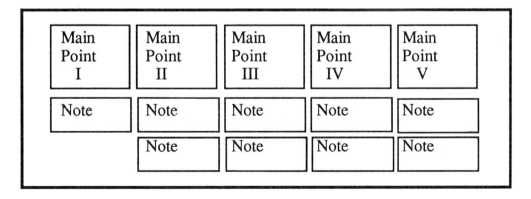

Make sure that you have information on every point, and that all points help to prove your hypothesis. Is any information brought up by two authors? Do they agree with each other? In either case, paper clip the two cards together. Do any notes pertain to two consecutive Main Point Cards? If so, place these cards at the end of the earlier Main Point line; you can potentially use them as transition sentences to smooth the way to the next point.

Experiment by moving the cards around, adding and removing cards until you are satisfied that 1) each notecard helps prove the main point at the top of the line and 2) that the order in which you have placed the notecards provides the best and most logical development of that main point.

It's All Coming Together Now — Making An Outline

If you have to hand an outline in to your teacher, slip a piece of carbon paper between two sheets of paper to make two copies at the same time. You will use your copy to work from while awaiting your teacher's OK.

Write your hypothesis on the first few lines. Underneath the hypothesis write I. Introduction. Each notecard under this Main Point Card is a capital letter, or if it is a subdivision of a capital letter, an Arabic numeral. Proceed through all the main points in the same way. Add a conclusion as your last Roman numeral. The model below shows you how your outline should look.

SAMPLE OUTLINE

Hypothesis: The election of Abraham Lincoln as president led to the outbreak of the Civil War.

I. Introduction

    A. brief background on tensions of time
    B. hypothesis statement
    C. Southern views of slavery and states' rights could not be
       squared with Lincoln's, therefore, his election led to the final
       North-South break

II. The slave-holding states

    A. views on slavery and states' rights
    B. how strong were these views?

III. Lincoln

A. his views on slavery and the Constitution
B. how strong were these views?

IV. Election of 1860

   A. what were the issues in the election?
   B. what were his statements on slavery and the constitution during the election campaign?

V. The election of Lincoln made further compromise impossible and war inevitable

   A. Southern reaction to the election of Lincoln
     1. thought Lincoln would not compromise further
     2. the South saw no way out but to go to war

   B. the North was in no mood for further compromise

VI. Conclusion

   A. views of North & South so far apart that clash inevitable
   B. election of Lincoln symbol that further compromise impossible
   C. therefore Lincoln's election led to Civil War

Now you have a wonderful outline. All the information is organized. If you find that there are still points on which you need more information, you need to go back to the library again. That will be a snap; you are already familiar with the place.

Writing the Paper

The First Draft

You will be writing at least three drafts, so the primary object of draft one is to get something down on paper. Do not worry about perfect spelling or stylistic elegance yet; these will come in later drafts. (You do not have to go out of your way to misspell words, though.) Since your first draft will need correction and revision, you need to make sure that you leave yourself ample room to make corrections on your first draft. Write on one side of the paper only, use pencil to make erasing easy, double space, and leave room at the top and bottom of the page. This procedure may waste a little paper, but it makes things much easier when you start correcting draft 1 and writing draft 2.

A research paper is traditionally divided into three parts: an introduction, where "you tell 'em what you will tell 'em;" the body of the paper, which "tells 'em;" and a conclusion, which "tells 'em what you told 'em."

The introduction, which should not be longer than one or two paragraphs, lays the groundwork for the paper. It is best to go from the general to the specific. Start off with the background, or larger picture, into which your paper fits. Now state your hypothesis. Your introduction should finish with the main points of your argument, the evidence with which you are demonstrating that your hypothesis is correct.

When writing the introduction, you might find it easiest to start in the middle. Begin with the hypothesis, which you already have on your outline. Next, put down the major points of proof. What you are really doing is converting the Roman numerals of your outline (except for the introduction and conclusion) to sentence form. Finally, describe in three or four sentences the background a non-expert reader will need to understand your hypothesis. When you are satisfied that the separate parts say what you want them to say, cut and tape them into the correct order.

The body of the paper contains the evidence you have gathered to prove the hypothesis. You need to explain to the reader how the evidence you have found (your notes) proves your hypothesis. In the body of your paper, you need to make the reader "see" what you "saw" and understand what you understand, so you need to present enough evidence and explain in enough detail to convince the reader, who is usually your teacher. All the evidence you present must be on the topic, that is, contribute to proving the hypothesis. If it does not, no matter how interesting it is, throw it out.

Your outline, or course, lists the points in the order in which you decided they had to be arranged to prove your hypothesis. In some ways it is easiest to write your paper in this order, although you do not absolutely have to work on the various points in the order they are listed in your outline. If you find it easier, start with the point you are most familiar with, find the appropriate cards and start writing. Just be sure to label the point you are working on clearly on each page and number the pages, so it will be easy to put the parts into the correct order later. Proceed point by point through the body of the paper, each time getting the appropriate cards out before you start.

As you write, you will need to indicate where the footnotes or endnotes will go in the finished paper, but you do not yet need the correct form. All you need to do at this stage is to put a short form of the bibliographic information and page number(s) (e.g. Jones, 54) in parentheses at the point where the reference is made. (Footnotes and endnotes supply the same information; they are just placed in different spots in the finished paper.)

This is a good place to discuss what sorts of things require a foot or endnote in a research paper. There are two reasons for having notes: They tell the reader where you got the information on which you are basing your hypothesis, and they let a reader know where he or she might get more detailed information on some aspects of your topic. While the second reason is a sort of service to the reader, the first reason is a form of intellectual honesty. The notes enable the reader to look up the specific pages of your sources that led you to the conclusion you stated in your paper. You are acknowledging where you got the basis for your own conclusions. The assumption if you have not cited a source is that you yourself thought this up. So if you do not cite your sources you are guilty of plagiarism, a serious academic offense. A plagiarist claims ideas or information, as his or her own, which he or she actually got from someone else.

What does all this mean in practice? Where do you actually have to put notes in your text? Essentially any summary, paraphrase, or direct quotation must be footnoted or endnoted. You do not have to footnote or endnote information that a "generally educated reader" would know, as for example, that George Washington was the first American President, or that Paris is the capital of France.

The function of the conclusion, which should be no longer than one paragraph, is to restate the hypothesis and the major points (the Roman numerals of your final outline) that proved your hypothesis. The conclusion should present no new material, and not ask any questions, but since the reader is now familiar with your proofs, you can restate your points using more sophisticated words than you used in the introduction.

If you wrote the body of the paper in segments that were not in order, put the pages of your first draft in proper order.

Writing The Second And Third Drafts

You should budget at least one hour per assigned page for this difficult stage of writing a research paper. If at all possible, let the first draft sit for twenty-four hours before starting on the second draft; allowing a little time to elapse makes it much easier to spot errors and make improvements. However, there is no reason to be idle during this "rest period." The paper is resting, not you. Use the time to finish some of the "mechanical things" that always seem to take more time than you have when the last hectic stage of research paper writing comes.

First type the title page. Your teacher will tell you what is required (usually the title of the paper, the teacher's name, your own name as author, the name of the course, and the date).

Second, alphabetize your bibliography cards according to author's last name, and type up the bibliography in proper form. Make sure to include all sources that are in footnotes, along with any others from which you got important material.

If your teacher lets you use the new form of citation, you can take a rest now. If you have to use the traditional style for foot or endnotes, use this time to write out the complete first citations for each of the sources you are using in your foot or endnotes on a piece of scrap paper. Remember, in the first draft of your paper you only used the short form. (After the first time any source is cited, you use the short form, which is not so much trouble.)

The first foot or endnotes citation presents the same information as the bibliography does, but in a somewhat different format. If your teacher gave you a style sheet, follow it. If not, follow the format given below. For types of sources not covered, ask your teacher or consult the book the experts use: Kate L.Turabian, *Student's Guide for Writing College Papers.*. Write all the first citations on a separate sheet of paper. That way, when you write the second draft you can save time; because you only need to cut the first citation off your sheet, tape it onto the page you are writing your footnotes or endnotes on, and add the foot or endnote number plus the specific pages you used.

SAMPLE TRADITIONAL STYLE FIRST FOOTNOTE OR ENDNOTE CITATIONS AS THEY WILL LOOK IN DRAFT 2

1. Encyclopedia Britanica, 25th ed. (1986), "The Civil War," by Jeremy Smith, 441-45.

2. Phillip Yardstick, Lincoln's Speeches (New York: Buchanon Publishing Co., 1985), p. 54.

3. Robert Bigtime, Lincoln: A Biography (Chicago, IL: Cross & White, 1979), p. 230.

4. Michael Jones, ed., Slavery and the Civil War (New York: McKinley Publishing Co., 1978), p. 6.

5. William Wisecrack, "The Election of 1860," Northern Historical Review 26 (April 1980): 332.

6. James Standish, Slavery and the American South (New York: Oak Publishing, 1977), p. 76.

7. Interview with Prof. James Book, an expert on Lincoln, University of Small Town, 12 June 1990.

After a day, you are ready to take up your paper again. Read the first draft aloud to someone else and have them ask questions. Make check marks and write a brief explanation in the margin at places where 1) you stumbled when reading (usually a place where the language or thought needs improving), 2) you or the listener had difficulty understanding what you meant 3) you or the listener could think of other improvements.

Once you have determined what needs changing or improving, write the new version between the lines, or move the material to another place, by cutting and taping. Try to produce a copy that someone else can follow.

Begin by making the changes that either you or the person you read draft 1 to suggested. Remember, you wrote notes in the margin when you read the first draft aloud. Next, work through draft 1 and make changes until all of the questions below can be answered with "yes."

1. Did you follow the outline in developing the hypothesis?
2. Does each paragraph contribute to proving the hypothesis?
3. Is everything in the most effective place?

Next, turn to the style. Again go over the paper sentence by sentence and make corrections or improvements until all of the questions below can be answered with "yes."
1. Does each paragraph have a topic sentence?
2. Do the other sentences in each paragraph develop the topic sentence

or provide a transition to the next paragraph?
3. Are all of the sentences as effective and concise as you can make them?
4. Do the words you use help the reader picture what you are describing?
5. Are there transitions between paragraphs and sections so the reader can follow your thoughts easily?

Now, work on grammar and spelling. Go through the whole paper again and make the necessary corrections until you are sure the grammar is correct and all of the words spelled right. For example, in checking your grammar, make sure all singular subjects have singular verbs. In terms of spelling, look up any words you are not sure of, and ask a good speller to correct any spelling errors you missed. Computer users, run the file through a spell checker.

Finally, old-style foot or endnote people have to fix up the mechanics. You are going to be glad that you do not have to spend time writing out the first citations at this point, since you did this when you let the first draft "rest." First number your foot or endnotes in the paper consecutively (using a red pen makes them easier to see). Then do the final preparation of your foot or endnotes on a separate piece of paper. Even if your teacher requires footnotes in the final paper, having them written in the form of endnotes at this stage helps you leave the right amount of space at the bottom of the page when you type the final draft of your paper. Do each note in turn, taking the first citation and taping it on the endnote sheet after the note number. Add the page number(s) you are citing and that note is finished. After the first citation only a short form and page number for any citation of the same source is required. If two or more notes in a row are from the same source, use *ibid*. (which means "the same" in Latin). The example below shows you how the foot or endnotes should look, as well as the proper use of "*ibid*." and the shortened form.

---

1. Phillip Yardstick, Lincoln's Speeches (New York: Buchanon Publishing Co., 1985), p. 54.

2. Ibid., p. 76.

3. William Wisecrack, "The Election of 1860," *Northern Historical Review* 26 (April 1980): 332.

4. Yardstick, Lincoln, p. 344.

Your second draft is now complete. Read the entire paper aloud to yourself to check for mistakes. Improve any spots that you cannot read smoothly. Give someone else your second draft to read and ask that kind person to make sure that all of the questions on content and style can be answered with "yes." Ask your reader to watch out for grammatical and spelling errors as well.

Make any of the suggested corrections you feel are necessary. Finally, type or print out the final version of your paper. If you are using footnotes, be sure to leave enough room at the bottom of the page. Assemble the parts of the paper in their proper order; using a plastic folder makes an effective presentation. Then, as a final step before handing in your paper, be sure to proofread it with a spell checker if you have one (perfect typists are rare) and make any last-minute corrections using white-out and matching black ink.

You are done!! Hand your paper in **on time** with a sigh of relief and a smile.

REFERENCES

Kuhlthau, Carol Collier. *Teaching the Library Research Process.* West Nyack, NY: Center for Applied Research in Education, 1985.

Turabian, Kate L. *Student's Guide for Writing College Papers.* 3rd. ed. Chicago: University of Chicago Press, 1976.

INDEX

Algebra, 31, 33-37
  assignment, 33, 36-37
  checking answer, 36, 39
  definition cards, 32, 44, 46
  homework, 31, 33-37, 44
  reading, 34
  review, 36
  sample problems, 34, 36-37
  study strategy, 33-37
  tests:
    studying for, 46-48
    taking, 49-50
  textbook, 34
  (*see also* Mathematics)
Aronson, Trudy, 127
Assignment, 1, 11, 14-15
  homework, 33, 39, 105, 136, 141, 158
  research papers, 179-80, 184
  and studying for tests, 46, 73, 105, 142, 144, 169-70
Attention, 5-6, 16
  in class, 44-45, 57, 82, 85, 99-100, 166-68
  task-oriented, 4-5
Attitude, 2, 4-7, 15-16
  "can do" student, 5, 18
  classroom behavior, 6, 15-18, 100, 166-68
  effort, 4, 6
    in history, 81, 85, 113
    in foreign language, 155, 169
    in science, 57
  frustration avoidance, 7-8
    in English, 127
    in foreign language, 163, 170
    in history, 82, 105-06
    in mathematics, 34-35, 37, 40
    in science, 67
  getting "unstuck," 5-6, 28, 164
  giving up, 5, 28
  good student behavior, 5-11, 18
  "study crunch," avoidance of, 11-14, 72-73
  "tuning in," 6-7, 15, 43-44, 71, 139, 167-68
  work habits, 7-8, 81-82

Bold print words (terms):
  in history, 81, 87-91, 95, 99, 101, 105
  in science, 57, 62, 64, 66-67, 70, 72

Brainstorming, 129-30, 134, 137, 180, 184
Brewer's Dictionary of Phrase and Fable, 122

"Caliban at Sunset," 124-25
Chute, Richard, 122
Classics, 122
Classroom behavior, 7, 17-18, 139, 166-68
Classwork:
  active listening, 100, 104
  asking questions, 67, 70-71, 76, 81, 99-100, 140
  boredom with, 6, 100, 139
  conflict with teacher, 3-4, 17-18
  and discussion, 14, 16, 23, 139-40
  in English, 139ff
  and feedback, 5, 71, 167
  in foreign language, 166ff, 177
  function of, 45
  in history, 100ff
  in mathematics, 27, 43ff, 51
  participation in, 16-18, 23
    in English, 139-41
    in foreign language, 167-68
Color, use of, 13
  in English, 144
  in foreign language, 159ff
  in history, 93, 106
  in science, 62, 66, 68
Concentration, 10, 14-15, 166-67
Context clues, 60, 89, 176

Definitions, 32, 40, 47, 53, 87
Dictionary, use of, 59-60, 90, 122, 157
Directions, reading of:
  in English, 134
  in foreign languages, 185
  in history, 81, 114, 147-48
  in mathematics, 49
  in science, 67-69, 77
  on tests, 1, 20-21, 49, 113, 147-48

Encyclopedia, use of, 84, 115, 121, 184
Endnotes (*see* Research paper)
English, 115ff
  brainstorming, 129-30, 134
  classwork, 139ff
  classics, reading of, 122

drafts, correction of, 132, 135-36, 139
grammar, 117, 126-28, 141-42, 148-49
homework, 119ff
images, 125-26
language, use in, 116-17, 138
literary terms, glossary of, 150-51
notetaking, 120, 140
novels, 116, 119-22
"personal textbook," 126-28
plays, 122-23
plot, 116, 120, 140, 142
poetry, 123-26, 136-39
"power words," 118, 120, 123, 135
reading techniques, 119-22, 125-26
short stories, 116, 119ff, 133-36
tests, 142ff
themes, 117, 128ff
vocabulary, 143-45, 148-49
and word processors, 115, 117, 134
English Grammar Digest, 127, 161
English Grammar for Students of French,
155, 161
Errors:
in foreign language, 167
in mathematics, 28, 36, 44, 50
in research paper, 198
in science, 66-68
Errors and Expectations, 18
Essay questions, 22
in English, 147-48
in history, 95-99, 106
in science, 77-79
(*See also* Taking tests)
Experiments (*See* Science)

Faulkner, William, 134
Footnotes (*See* Research paper)
Foreign language, 155ff
classwork, 166ff, 177
communication in, 154
culture, 154, 165, 171
cumulative nature of, 155, 157
dictation, 175-76
directions, 158
exercizes, 158, 163-64
errors, 167
grammar, 154-55, 157, 161-63, 166, 170
homework, 154ff, 168
Latin, 154, 164
learning environment, 157
listening, 177ff
memorizing, 160-61, 170
multi-sensory learning, 158-60, 162-64

oral work, 174-75
"own text," 163-64, 170-71
pronunciation, 155, 159, 161, 163-64
reading, 154-55, 163-64, 176-77
review, 165-66, 168ff
speaking, 157, 174-75
spelling, 175-76
tapes, 167-68
tests:
studying for, 169-72
taking, 172-74
thinking in, 159, 166-67
translation of, 164-65
vocabulary, 154-55, 158-61, 165-66,
170, 175
workbook, 174
writing in, 175-76

Geometry, 39ff (*See also* Mathematics)
assignment sheet, 39, 46
classwork, 43-45
definitions, 32, 40, 43-44, 46
diagrams, 41-42
homework, 39-43
proofs, 42-43
review, 43-44, 46-48
theorem cards, 40-44, 47
tests:
studying for, 46-48
taking, 49-50
Glossary:
in history, 85
in science, 53, 57
of literary terms, 150-51
Grammar:
in English, 117, 126-28, 141-42, 148-49
in foreign languages, 154-55, 157, 161-
63, 166, 170
and research paper, 198
Graphics (*See* Visual aids)

Hemingway, Ernest, 134
Highlighting:
in English, 143, 145
in history, 86, 91, 106, 108-09
in science, 66-67
History, 81ff
classwork, 82, 100ff, 107-08, 113
difficulties in, 84
highlighting in, 86, 91, 106, 108-09
homework, 85ff
bold print terms, 81, 87-88
and notetaking, 90ff, 101-03

"people, events, dates" list, 92-93, 99
"question words," 94
and textbook reading, 86-90
language, use of, 84, 88
and lecture format, 101-03
retention, 87, 91, 101, 104, 108
review, 100-01, 104ff, 107-08, 113
tests:
    studying for, 104ff
    taking, 112-13
textbook, 84, 86ff, 90ff, 113
writing in, 95-98, 106-07, 112-13
(*See also* Research paper)
Homework, 5, 9, 15-16, 18, 23
in English, 119ff
in foreign languages, 154ff
in history, 85ff
in mathematics, 31ff
in science, 57ff

Improving Reading in Every Class, 3, 5,
28, 45, 66, 169
Index, use of, 33, 85, 157, 191

Laboratory:
experiments, 55, 65-68, 79
reports, 69-70, 76, 78-79
(*See also* Science)
Language, use of:
in history, 84, 88
in literature, 116-17, 120, 123, 138
in mathematics, 29, 50
in science, 54, 69, 79
Latin language, 54, 58-59, 79, 154, 164
Lecture format, 54-55, 70-72, 79
Library, use of, 181ff, 187-88 (*See also*
Research paper)
Listening:
active, 16, 18, 101, 104
as aid to comprehension, 37-38, 64, 144
during lecture, 70-71
in foreign language, 167, 177
to sounds and rythm of words, 125-26,
138
to teacher, 14-15, 17, 23
Little things that help, 1, 4, 8
in English, 115
in foreign language, 153
in history, 81
in mathematics, 27
in science, 53

Mathematics, 27ff (*See also* Algebra,

Geometry)
checking answers, 36-39, 50
classwork, 43-45
cumulative nature of, 29, 34, 46, 51
difficulties, in, 28-30
graphics, 33, 38, 42
language, use in, 29
reading, 29, 31-34, 39-40, 50
technical terms, 29
tests:
    studying for, 45-48
    taking, 48-50
textbook, study of, 31-33, 39
theorems, 40ff
vocabulary in, 31-32
word problems, 37-39
Memorizing, 64-65, 75, 108, 143-44,
160-61, 170
"Mini-outlines," 78, 113, 147
Multi-sensory learning:
in English, 143-44
in foreign languages, 158-60, 162-64
in history, 108-09
in science, 65

National Geographic, 53
Notecards (*See* Research paper)
Notetaking, 11, 15-17
in English, 120, 140
in history, 90ff, 101-04
for research paper, 179, 183ff, 188-91
in science, 63-64, 70-72, 79
(*See also* Highlighting, Outlining)

Oral communication, 174-75
Organization, 8ff, 23
in writing, 109-12, 128ff, 147-48
of notecards, 191-92
of study materials, 1, 9-12, 14, 15
of study space, 1, 9-10
of study time, 8ff, 30-33, 51, 72, 105
Outlining, 92-93, 109-11, 130-31, 186,
192-94

Paragraphs:
in essay questions, 78, 107
structure of, 86, 131-32
Paraphrasing, 189
Parts of speech (*See* English, grammar;
and Foreign language, grammar)
Periodicals, 182-83
Phonetic rules, 59-60, 176
Plagiarism, 133, 189, 195-97 (*See also*